Enhancing Joy in Travel

Enhancing Joy in Travel

Removing Obstacles to Satisfaction

Virginia Murphy-Berman

BEP
BUSINESS EXPERT PRESS
Leader in applied, concise business books

First published in 2021 by
Business Expert Press, LLC
222 East 46th Street, New York, NY 10017
www.businessexpertpress.com

ISBN-13: 978-1-94944-321-9 (paperback)
ISBN-13: 978-1-94944-322-6 (e-book)

Business Expert Press Tourism and Hospitality Management Collection

Collection ISSN: 2375-9623 (print)
Collection ISSN: 2375-9631 (electronic)

First edition: 2021

10 9 8 7 6 5 4 3 2 1

Description

Why do so many people love to travel, but sometimes come away unhappy and disappointed in their trips? What can people in the travel industry do to prevent such discontent and promote optimal travel experiences? As a clinical psychologist and an avid traveler, I wanted to write a book that offers fresh perspectives on these questions.

Readers will learn a new way of thinking about the nature of travel and about solutions to common travel problems. Strategies informed by psychological theory and research that travel providers can use to enhance their clients' positive travel encounters are given.

Questions explored include: How do travelers' personalities impact travel satisfaction? Why can seeking perfection in travel and trying to keep up with the often-unrealistic depictions of travel on social media undermine travel joy? What can be done to overcome travel fatigue and boredom? How can travelers prepare for trips in ways that spark excitement and receptivity for what is to come? And what can enhance the enjoyment trips give travelers long after their trips are over?

This book is a must read for those in the hospitality and travel industry (both students and professionals) and general readers who want to better understand the complexities of the psychology of travel. It will serve as an invaluable guide to all who would like to learn what it means to travel well.

Keywords

travel; tourist industry; hospitality industry; travelers; tourists; stages of travel; art of travel anticipation; travel receptivity; travel reminiscing and reflecting; personality and travel; character strengths and travel; big data; customization of travel; travel as experience; happiness; well-being; savoring; person-environment fit

Contents

Preface ix

Acknowledgments xi

Introduction xiii

Section I   **Setting the Stage** 1

Chapter 1   Travel Over Time 3
Chapter 2   Travel at Its Best 7

Section II   **Achieving Positive Travel Outcomes** 13

Part I   *Pre-Trip Anticipation* 15

Chapter 3   Setting Expectations 17
Chapter 4   Increasing Trip Readiness 23
Chapter 5   Fostering Pre-Trip Excitement 29
Chapter 6   Facilitating Environmental Fit I 35
Chapter 7   Facilitating Environmental Fit II 43
Case Study 1   Pre-Trip Anticipation 50

Part II   *The Actual Trip* 53

Chapter 8   Ameliorating Travel Fatigue 55
Chapter 9   Mitigating Comparison Tendencies 63
Chapter 10   Reducing Travel Habituation I 71
Chapter 11   Reducing Travel Habituation II 77
Chapter 12   Facilitating Use of Time 83
Chapter 13   Promoting Traveler Engagement 89
Chapter 14   Enhancing Experiences of Awe 95
Case Study 2   The Actual Trip 99

Part III   *Post-Trip Well-Being* 101

Chapter 15   Supporting Use of Mementos 103
Chapter 16   Helping Travel Story Sharing 109
Chapter 17   Promoting Travel Journaling 113

Chapter 18   Assisting in Post-Trip Knowledge Extension 117
Case Study 3 Post-Trip Well-Being 121

The End 123
References 125
About the Author 137
Index 139

Preface

We live in times of great material wealth and abundance where we have an unprecedented number of options available to us to add convenience to our daily lives. Interestingly, at this same time that we have so many ways to make our lives more comfortable at home, we have actually been spending more and more money on traveling away from home. Although there may be some changes in how and why we travel in the aftermath of the coronavirus pandemic, the psychological needs that travel fulfills are not likely to be greatly altered. Travel is not something we do to get away from our lives, but rather something we pursue to fully embrace life. We may travel a bit differently in the future, but the joy in the memorable experiences it can bring will not be diminished. This is the case whether our trips take us only a few miles away from our homes or halfway around the world.

Because travel is so important to us, I wanted to write a book that would help us better savor the benefits it can provide. I bring my own considerable experience with domestic and world travel to this topic and the opportunities that I have had to live for different periods in a variety of foreign countries. Through these encounters, I have personally witnessed some of the best and the worst that travel has to offer. I have seen how travel can immeasurably improve our lives, and I have observed how truly disastrous some trips can be.

In addition to my personal experience with travel, I also bring to this topic my longtime work as a clinical psychologist and a professor who has taught and done research on what promotes a sense of well-being in life. Through my studies and discussions with students in classroom debates on this topic, I learned that happiness is often derived not from the big things that happen to us in life, but rather from daily, small occurrences that take place and that touch us in some special way. This is true in travel, as well, and we will come back to this idea again and again as we explore what causes our trips to be either joyful encounters or disappointing failures.

In all of this, there will be an appreciation that what we, as travelers, are looking for is not cookie-cutter sameness, but rather something that feels real and vivid that is addressed uniquely to us. This book will examine how we and travel providers alike can work collaboratively to facilitate this goal. When it is achieved, travel can become truly magical.

Acknowledgments

I would like to acknowledge my husband, John, for so patiently putting up with me during the time I spent working on this book. I say this fully aware that a person writing a book is not always the easiest person to be around. John has been my partner on a great number of travel journeys, and many of the stories in this book reflect some of the wonderful experiences we have had together on our trips. Besides being my favorite travel companion, John is also my best writing critic and my most supportive sounding board for ideas. He read numerous draft versions of this book, and his comments and suggestions made my work much stronger. I have no words to thank him enough for that.

Introduction

The real voyage of discovery consists not in seeking new landscapes, but in having new eyes.

—Marcel Proust

Over the past years, more and more of us have traveled for pleasure and business than ever before. Tourism has, in fact, become a huge world-wide industry. For instance, data from the World Tourism Organization (UNWTO 2020) indicated that in 2019 there were 1.5 billion people who traveled internationally. This represented a four percent increase from the previous year and a 68-fold increase from data available in 1950 (Roser 2020). Not only were more of us traveling, in general, but we were taking more frequent trips throughout our lifetimes (Opperman 1995), with many of us embarking on more than one holiday per year. Export earnings generated from travel are significant, topping 1.7 trillion dollars in 2019 (UNWTO 2019). Of course, the current coronavirus pandemic has temporarily interfered with our ability to travel, and how that will alter travel patterns in the future is unknown. What is clear is that the desire for travel will never diminish, nor will our wanderlust to explore our world decrease. Travel is a dream for a significant number of us that will never die. While many of our trips are undoubtedly very enjoyable, a significant number fail to live up to the often unrealistically high expectations we have for them. Many of us, in truth, are sometimes secretly disappointed that our dream vacations are not always completely perfect, or we feel a sense of letdown after our much-anticipated trips are over and we have to go back to our pre-trip lives. This may occur despite the fact that we are spending more and more money on traveling than ever before (Fox 2019), and more and more resources are available to help us plan our trips (Adams 2016).

In this book, we talk about why we may so often be disappointed even with seemingly picture-perfect travel agendas and the most wonderful travel accommodations. This is a book about how we and those in the travel industry can work together to curtail this disappointment and maximize positive travel experiences. It is a book about the kinds of behavior and thinking that people (both travelers and travel providers) often engage in during traveling that either promote satisfaction and happiness or lead to discontent and misery. We explore what can be done to increase the happiness and decrease the discontent. Our exploration will be grounded in research from the fields of tourism studies and positive psychology, the latter of which looks at the conditions under which individuals experience optimal functioning and flourishing in life (Gable and Haidt 2005; Seligman 2011).

At its heart, traveling well is all about increasing our responsiveness to what is positive in our surroundings and enhancing our ability to encounter authentic moments. Guaranteeing success in travel is not about creating ideal places or the most exotic travel environments. Rather, it is about learning how to build settings and promote experiences that allow us to thrive on our own terms.

Structure of the Book

The book is divided into two main sections and 18 chapters. In Section I, which serves as a foundational base for the rest of the book, a brief overview of the background and history of travel is given, and the nature of the positive travel outcomes that we seek are defined.

In Section II, we turn to an examination of how achievement of the outcomes for travel discussed in Section I can best be facilitated by those in the travel industry and to an analysis of what types of obstacles have to be overcome to make this happen. This second section is presented in three parts, each with multiple chapters. In Part I, the anticipatory phase of travel is explored, and ways that travel providers can work with us to help make this aspect of travel positive and productive are discussed. In Part II, strategies that travel providers can use to increase our satisfaction during our actual trip experiences are examined. The post-trip experience is turned to last in Part III.

Throughout the book, questions for discussion and hypothetical case study problems are included. The purpose of these exercises is to facilitate your ability to make links and connections between the chapter material and your own experiences, either as a traveler or as someone in the travel industry. There are no right or wrong answers to these questions or case studies. Rather, they are provided to help you extend and apply the theories and concepts that you read about to real-life travel issues. Working on them will deepen your understanding of the key ideas in the book, so they should not be skipped!

We will start with a general overview of travel in Chapter 1.

SECTION I

Setting the Stage

CHAPTER 1

Travel Over Time

(or I Never Understood Why My Ancestors Hated Being on the Road So Much!)

The world is a book and those who do not travel only read one page.
—St. Augustine

Travel: What is the Purpose?

As we begin to consider the idea of travel, it is helpful to start with a brief reflection on why people travel at all. Probably every one of us has a different explanation for why we either love or hate traveling. As we have briefly discussed, the rewards of travel can be glorious, but the agonies can be gut-wrenching as well. Given this, we might ask why we even bother with travel unless it is completely necessary. Why don't we just stay home as much as possible and buy more and more products to increase our comfort and pleasure? We could purchase a cozy bed, buy a great TV, stock our pantries with food, acquire a nice fluffy robe and so on, and just relax in our homes. Certainly, if we wanted to learn about the world and foreign places or see beautiful sights, we could simply tune in to a variety of travel or nature shows and never have to get up out of our chairs.

This then is the question. What are we looking for that is so important that we will put up with all of the hassles and irritants that mark modern travel? Why do we willingly leave the comfort of our homes to set out on journeys to distant places to seek something where outcomes are uncertain and rewards are often intangible? And why did people travel in the past when being *on the road* was probably even more potentially perilous than it is now? To consider these kinds of questions, let's first talk briefly about the nature of travel and how it has changed over time.

Travel Today and Yesterday

To our distant ancestors, the notion of traveling undoubtedly had a very different meaning than it does for us today. Travel then was often not just emotionally challenging and tiresome, but also physically exhausting and quite dangerous. Few people had the means or even the desire to roam the world far away from their homes. Further, when people did travel, their goals were usually quite instrumental and specific. For instance, people traveled to locate food sources in times of famine, or they set out for religious reasons on holy pilgrimages to sacred shrines. Some traveled in order to promote trade, or to try to recover from illness by visiting so-called healing places (Csikszentmihaly and Coffey 2016). What people did *not* do nearly as much as in the present time, though, was travel for the sheer fun of it. This reason, in fact, would probably have never even occurred to most ancient people. Of course, now we travel for many reasons that would appear strange to our ancestors, and the things that give us satisfaction in travel are quite diverse (Chen, Mak and McKercher 2011; Moscardo 2011). For instance, we travel for what have been called *push* reasons such as the desire to escape or to get away from the pressures of modern life. We also travel for more external *pull* reasons such as the chance to experience great adventures or to encounter beautiful places or simply to relax (see Crompton 1979; Andersen, Prentice and Watanabe 2000). Regardless of our specific motives, however, most of us want to travel today to achieve some types of memorable experiences (Bowen and Clarke 2009; Pearce 2005; Schmitt 2003). This is important. It reflects a shift in how travel has been construed from being a tiresome burden we have to carry out for practical reasons to something we want to do to live our lives more fully. But why is having memorable experiences so important to us, and why are they so sought after? Let's turn to that question next.

Travel as Experience

Research suggests that we often gain more pleasure from actively experiencing things than passively consuming products (Van Boven and

Gilovich 2003). Experiences give us a deeper feeling of satisfaction and provide us with more of a sense of meaning and accomplishment (see Pine and Gilmore 1998, for a discussion of the experience economy). In fact, some have suggested that what is most important these days is not so much what particular services or goods are offered to us, but rather what we can *do* with these goods and services, or how creatively we can interact with them (Pine and Gilmore 2019). For instance, when we travel instead of simply wanting to be passive participants on a tour, more and more of us desire to be directly and actively involved in a variety of tour activities. This means that in addition to simply listening to a talk on how to make a certain type of bread given by a local guide on some excursion to Germany, many of us appreciate having a chance to try out the bread-making process ourselves. We also increasingly like to have choices about what we see and do, and in this sense, often love occasions where we can co-create our experiences with our travel providers (Mackenzie and Kerr 2013). As an example, imagine a situation in which a tour guide takes a group of us to a certain famous garden in some area because she has learned that several people in our group have a particular interest in plants and flowers. In this instance, both we and our tour guide co-determine the travel agenda together.

Many of us, thus, want more participatory involvement in the process of travel itself. This is the case whether we are searching for highly energetic travel adventures or more quiet and serene experiences of rest and escape. This is also the case whether we are embarking on more structured, organized group tours, or prefer setting out on our own to explore our world. Travel is increasingly becoming a dynamic, interactive encounter between our travel providers and us as we engage with each other to facilitate optimal travel outcomes. We will look more at this process of active engagement between us and our travel providers in subsequent chapters of this book as we continue to examine what it means to travel well.

Chapter 1: Questions for Discussion

Before we turn to new themes, though, in order to think more about the ideas presented in Chapter 1, please work on the following questions. As you answer these questions, draw on your own personal experiences and/or your experiences in some aspect of the travel industry.

1. How has travel changed over your lifetime? In what ways would you say it is different today than it was when you were a child? Is this a change for better or for worse? Discuss.

2. What does the idea of *memorable experience in travel* mean to you? Give some specific examples to support your answer.

3. As we have seen, many of us like to have more choices today over our travel venues than we did in the past and often appreciate chances to co-create experiences with our travel providers. Is this true in your own travel experience or the experience of others you have known? If yes, explain. What are the downsides of having more choices?

4. The idea of engaged versus more passive travel styles was also discussed briefly in this chapter. What sort of travel venues have you been involved with that particularly lent themselves to the creation of *engaged* travel opportunities? What does this idea mean to you? Explain.

Notes

_____

_____

_____

_____

_____

_____

CHAPTER 2

Travel at Its Best

(or Traveling Has Really Made My Life Better)

Certainly, travel is more than the seeing of sights; it is a change that goes on, deep and permanent, in the ideas of living.
—Mary Ritter Beard

Chapter Preview

In this chapter, the important benefits and rewards that travel can provide are discussed. These benefits range from concrete, practical gains such as learning a new language to more intangible psychological effects such as acquiring an expanded sense of self. All of these benefits can endure far beyond the actual timeframe of a specific trip and contribute to the power of travel to make a lasting, positive impact on our lives.

Definition of Who We Are

As we discussed, whether we embark on trips mostly to escape or mostly to find adventure, many of us want to encounter some kind of noteworthy experiences as we travel. But what are such experiences, and why are they so vital to us?

First, when they are particularly memorable, travel experiences can help define our sense of who we are as a person (Kurtz 2017; Filep, Laing and Csikszentmihalyi 2016) and can aid us in discovering key components of our identity. Experiences add to our narratives of ourselves. Research, in fact, has shown (Van Boven and Gilovich 2003) that when we are asked to tell others the story of our lives we rarely mention the things we owned or the square footage of the houses we purchased. We will, however, often bring up our memorable experiences, including our travel experiences. For example, we might talk about the time we went to China or the time we swam in the Caribbean and saw a dolphin, and so on. These sorts of experiences stay with us and are used to build our personal histories and expand our self-definitions. This is especially the case when we have had experiences that we perceive to be very authentic or that reflect our core ideas of ourselves (Desforges 2000).

To consider this more, imagine that on a vacation we had the chance to utilize all of our physical, mental, and emotional powers to successfully climb a particularly challenging mountain range. The experience of doing this could forever after alter how we think about ourselves, and in our minds we may now seem stronger or more courageous than we were before. On the other hand, if we had simply stayed at home and passively watched someone else climb this same mountain on TV, our expanded sense of self would be much less likely to occur.

Such self-expansion can also emerge from doing things during traveling that are not as daunting as climbing a challenging mountain range. For instance, after visiting a foreign city, we might gain a heightened sense of efficacy from our ability to negotiate rides in a foreign subway system or to competently use money in a different currency. Although these may seem like small accomplishments, they can alter the way we view our capabilities and can add to new feelings of confidence and effectiveness.

It is interesting in this regard to note that when researchers have asked people to draw pictures of themselves that represent who they really are and then draw key material purchases and important experiences next to their self-depictions, experiences were often drawn closer to the self-drawings than material goods (Carter and Gilovich 2012). This suggests, as several researchers have put it so well (see Kumar, Killingsworth and Gilovich 2014), that at a deep level we are what we do, not what we own!

Need Satisfaction

Travel at its best can also satisfy deep cravings that are important in other ways to our psychological well-being. To achieve optimal functioning, according to Abraham Maslow (1943), we need to fulfill not just basic needs such as needs for safety or security, but also higher-order needs such as the need for esteem or self-actualization. Fulfilling these higher types of needs contributes to our sense of meaning and purpose in life, something that goes well beyond our search for simple survival. Although it is not always the case, traveling when it works can help us satisfy such needs by offering us chances for important expansive self-defining experiences (Kasser and Ryan 1996; Howell and Hill 2009). Thus, while our purchase of a great new winter coat satisfies our need for simple warmth and to be less exposed to the elements when we go outside, it does not fulfill a longing that we sometimes feel for something bigger in our lives that is larger than the mere desire for comfort (Maslow 1968). Our desire to satisfy this longing for something more can be as strong as our cravings for sugar or chocolate or salt. In fact, as many researchers have noted, true contentment in life comes from the satisfaction of both what are called hedonic and eudaemonic elements (Seligman 2002; Waterman 2008). The former concerns what we think of as pleasant sensations and sensory comforts. The latter entails opportunities to seek a kind of self-transcendence that is based on having deep and meaningful experiences (Delle Fave, Brdar, Freire, Vella-Brodrick and Wissing 2011; Felip and Pearce 2014). Travel, when it lives up to its name, can provide us with both these important aspects of well-being.

Social Connections to Others

Travel can additionally expand our external connections to others as we foster new and interesting relationships or cement old ones (Pearce, Filep and Ross 2011). We need and desire these kinds of connections to overcome core feelings of isolation and loneliness that can beset us at times and to forge the unique feelings of camaraderie that can come from having done something special with another person (Diener and Seligman 2002; Boothby, Clark and Bargh 2014). In fact, we do not always have to travel together or share an actual trip with another person to have these types of strong feelings of connections emerge. I can, for instance, feel a special kind of bonding with you when I learn that you also did something that was particularly memorable to me. I might say, "Oh...you too hiked in Nepal and went to Kathmandu" or "You too lived in Germany for a while or went to such and such a music festival." Recognition of these types of common experiences can facilitate a sense that we possess a certain kind of knowledge and understanding of the world that is less available to others (Caprariello and Reis 2013). Through this process, travel experiences can become a powerful glue that links us together.

Impact on Society: Increasing Social Capital

The experiences we accumulate through traveling can further positively impact others around us, although this important consequence of travel is sometimes forgotten (Coleman 1988). To give a personal example, when I had the opportunity to live abroad for a year, I came back and had the chance to talk to many friends and neighbors about my experiences and how travel changed my way of seeing things. People told me that my excitement and stories piqued their interest in traveling and introduced them to new ways of looking at and thinking about the world.

Travel also allows us to pick up concrete skills and competencies that we can pass on to others after our journeys are over. For instance, we might learn a new way of playing an instrument or tying a scarf to share with our friends when we return home. Or we might bring back creative and new types of musical recordings to listen to or new dance steps to try out. In all these ways, the social capital in society is increased, and we can help others grow in their understanding of the world. Travel, in this manner, often has a ripple effect in which change at one small level can bubble and expand over time to include a wider and wider range of people.

Where We Go From Here

For a variety of reasons, then, travel can add tremendously to our lives. But not all travel experiences will do this. If we do not prepare for our travels well they can disappoint us, or if we repeat the same experiences over and over, we can adapt to them just like we adapt to material objects. If we have experiences that do not fit us and our personality, we can feel put off by them. If experiences seem phony or artificial, the joy we take participating in them is diminished. These are some of the challenges of traveling well that we will continue to discuss in the next section of the book.

Questions for Discussion

Before we move on, please work with the following questions to think more about the benefits of travel and about the tremendous power it can have on our lives. Draw mainly on your personal experience as a traveler as you do this.

1. Think of completing "I am the kind of person who likes to...." type statements. When you consider such statements, are your self-descriptions influenced by any memorable experiences that you had when traveling somewhere? If yes, please describe.

2. Imagine meeting someone whom you knew nothing about. Do you think your conception of this person would change if they told you that they had traveled the world multiple times versus that they had never been out of their home town? Explain.

3. We, it seems, need to be connected to others to function at an optimal level. Think of this in terms of your own travel experiences or any experiences you have had in the travel industry. Do you think people get to know each other differently through traveling with them, as opposed to interacting with them in other settings? If you think this is the case, how or why is it so?

4. Think of the kinds of knowledge or skills either you, yourself, or someone you know acquired through traveling. Describe some of these.

Notes

_____

_____

_____

_____

_____

_____

SECTION II
Achieving Positive Travel Outcomes

PART I

Pre-Trip Anticipation

The pleasure isn't in doing the thing; the pleasure is in planning it.
—John Green

We have talked about the benefits that travel can provide. But the first step to ensuring good trip outcomes is knowing how to plan well. Planning and anticipating something, in fact, can sometimes be as thrilling as actually obtaining the thing that we desire. This experience of anticipation is the first part of savoring (Bryant and Veroff 2007), and when applied to traveling, it allows us to prolong pleasure in our trip experiences. To do this, though, we have to expand in our minds how we think of the whole idea of waiting and getting ready.

We will look at some of the features of positive anticipation and trip preparation in the next five chapters. A major step in creating such positive anticipation has to do with being able to prepare for our trips in ways that match our own personal preparation and information-seeking styles. What makes us, indeed, feel ready for something, what makes us feel excited and hopeful, and what sparks our imaginative longings as we think about our future trips may be very different for us than it is for our friends or neighbors. We will learn why this is the case as we discuss how to maximize the trip planning process in a number of different ways. We will also examine some common roadblocks that can occur as we set our general trip goals and objectives in place, a subject we will turn to first in the next chapter.

CHAPTER 3

Setting Expectations

(or I Only Want a Completely Perfect Trip: Is That so Much to Ask?)

What makes earth feel like hell is our expectation that it should feel like heaven.

—Chuck Palahniuk

Chapter Preview

The importance of dreaming and then of setting realistic and achievable trip goals in the trip planning processes is discussed in this chapter. Common errors that we often make when thinking about our trip goals such as seeking perfection in our travels or trying to do too much in one trip are additionally examined, as well as strategies that a travel planner can use to help us avoid these roadblocks.

Trip Dreaming

The first part of planning a trip begins when we start to dream about different travel destination possibilities. Such dreaming, as we have noted, can be quite fun and can be a very pleasurable part of the anticipation process. We have to be careful, however, that our dreams reflect what we ourselves really want from our trips and are not based on unrealistic notions of what others have had or done. Dreams about travel can be fueled by multiple sources these days. For instance, we might look at pictures on Instagram or Facebook sent by a friend about the friend's vacation to some Hawaiian beach resort and immediately want to go to this resort ourselves. Or we might see a television ad featuring a large cruise line that offers passengers seemingly wonderful package tours to exotic locations and then decide that we must be on that cruise. The difficulty is that these images are carefully curated to show everyone and every location in the best possible light. Our friends, for instance, may happily provide us with beautifully posed images of themselves having a great time at a Hawaiian luau; they do not as readily, though, show pictures of themselves standing in a long line at the lost luggage counter at the airport. Thus, while exposure to inspiring images can help give us some ideas of different trip options, seeing only descriptions of the apparent endlessly incredible travel experiences of others can also distort our thinking. In this chapter we will talk more about how and why this is the case and then explore what those in the travel industry might do to help us consider our travel goals in ways that are more apt to lead to agreeable trip outcomes.

Maximizing Tendencies

One factor that often adds to our lack of satisfaction during traveling is the false idea that everything on our trip must be perfect (as it seems to have been for other people) or it will all be worthless. Let's consider this more.

When we spend lots of money and energy planning a dream trip, it seems straightforward enough that we would want everything about our trip to be the best possible. We want to eat the best food, to have a chance to gaze at the best sites, to take the best tours, and to participate in the most exciting and best adventures. This aim for perfection in everything is known as *maximizing* (Cheek and Schwartz 2016); and at first glance, it might seem like a good and worthwhile goal for all travelers to have. After all, why shouldn't everyone desire the highest standards in everything? Don't we all deserve it? Isn't this, at least, a good aspirational goal to hold? While the truth of this might seem intuitively obvious, we will see that constantly seeking out only the best can have some significant downsides (Iyengar, Wells and Schwartz 2006).

First, pursuing the best in everything on our future trips is probably an impossible goal to achieve. And even if we think we have reached perfection in our planning, the reality of our actual trips often turns out to be less perfect than the flawlessness of our plans. This is like the New Years' Eve conundrum. We often think so unrealistically about how wonderful New Year's Eve celebrations will be that the events of the evening itself turn out to be a severe letdown for many. Some of us remember the year 2000 millennium parties where the hype was simply too much for most people to live up to. Talking too much about or expecting perfection inevitably fuels anticlimax!

Another downside of searching for trip perfection is that seeking the perfect trip can evolve into a search not for what is best for us, but rather what is better than what others have. For instance, we may have reserved a beautiful room for our cruise, but then find much to our chagrin that our colleague at work, who took the same cruise the previous year, had secured an even better room for the same price. When best becomes *better than*, this kind of knowledge can lead to significant unhappiness.

Finally, when we desire perfection, we may begin to want the best of everything on our vacations not because we think we would especially enjoy this or that, but because by getting the best, we would prove to ourselves and others how smart and effective we are as people (Hughes and Scholer 2017). This becomes perilous because it basically puts our self-worth on the line with every trip we take, something that we all want to avoid.

As we think about all of the above, it is interesting to note that research has shown (Iyengar and Lepper 2000) that if we are maximizers we often do achieve objectively better outcomes than non-maximizers, but we end up being less satisfied with our results because we are always looking for something even greater around the corner. Needless to say, this makes efforts to find happiness from the pursuit of perfection doubly difficult to achieve.

Imposed Time Pressures

At the same time that we may feel compelled to search for the very best in everything, we also may feel pressure in our very fast-paced worlds to constantly do and achieve more and more. Good trips can then become defined as ones that are frenetically busy. This conceptualization of successful trips often leads to later travel dissatisfaction because it produces situations where we begin to simply check off sites and places we visited rather than taking the time to really see and appreciate them (Bryant and Veroff 2007). Unfortunately, if we succumb to these sorts of *do-it-all* pressures, we end up feeling simply tired rather than nourished and refreshed by our trips.

Facilitating Realistic Trip Planning

Maximizing tendencies and imposed time demands can, therefore, greatly interfere with our ability to plan satisfying trips. Because these biases and tendencies often play out under the radar of individual awareness, we are usually not conscious of *why* we think we must take this or that sort of trip, or *why* we are unexpectedly disappointed later when some of the actual trip experiences fail to live up to our initial dreams.

Helping us set more realistic trip goals is where a good travel planner can come into the picture. Travel planners can aid us in putting together optimal trip agendas by listening to the kinds of experiences we want to have. They can ascertain our interests and preferences for things like methods of travel and/or room accommodations and tastes in dining and then put together very personalized itineraries for us. They can also assist us in selecting destination sites (Hague 2016). To do all of this well, however, a travel planner has to be able to listen very carefully not only to *what* we say we want to experience, but also to *why* having these particular kinds of experiences seems so important and necessary to us. By listening for the *why* underneath the *what*, a planner can assess if we are unwittingly placing pressures on ourselves that could undermine the success of our trip experiences. Do we, for instance, seem to be seeking some kind of trip perfection that doesn't really exist? Have we obtained ideas about what we should do and experience from others who are conveying very unrealistic portrayals of travel bliss to us? Do we want to do too much on our trips, forgetting that transaction costs, including not only money but also time and energy and, perhaps, discomfort, must be dealt with as we navigate from one site to another? More generally, do we expect to experience continual joy while traveling without remembering all of the hassles and irritations that are also part of the travel process?

All of this means travel planners must explore not merely our desires and interests, but, in addition, talk with us about our energy level, need for downtime, tolerance for discomfort, and degree of patience we are likely to have if/when things go awry. Discussion of such topics would considerably aid us in identifying realistic travel motives and goals, and in this way satisfactory trips that are also doable and achievable would be more likely to emerge.

Travel providers could additionally show us possible travel venues from a variety of sources that go beyond paper brochures or conventional photos of travel sites. For instance, we could be shown reviews and even video montages from hotel websites that depict the kinds of experiences different guests have actually had during their stays at these hotels. Whatever they were, having a chance to be privy to these sorts of depictions could give us some valuable data about the types of encounters that might realistically await us in different sorts of travel environments. We could then use this to make more informed assessments about where we would be apt to feel most or least comfortable, or about what types of activities we might enjoy or not enjoy. Besides assisting us in making good general travel choices, with our permission, such information on our preferences could also be shared with travel professionals at our chosen travel destinations. This would allow them to arrange advance bookings for us for activities during our stays that are likely to be particularly suited to us. All of this would contribute to the chances that our chosen travel goals would lead to positive trip outcomes and not to disappointed dreams.

Questions for Discussion

In order to think more about how to set workable and realistic travel expectations and goals and about the factors that can sometimes impede this, please answer the following questions. Draw on both your personal experience and/or any experiences you have had in the travel industry as you do this.

1. Picture in your mind someone you would define as a maximizer (either yourself or someone you know). How does this tendency affect how you or this other person like(s) to prepare for trips? Explain.

2. Now think of someone (either yourself or someone you know) who seems to want to do everything in a hurry and to cram more and more activities into every moment. Again, consider how this tendency affects your own or this other person's travel preparation habits. Explain.

3. Ponder now some of the suggestions given in this chapter on how travel planners might work with those of us who have these maximizing or *want-to-do-it-all* tendencies. Did any of these suggestions stand out to you or seem particularly helpful? If yes, describe. Are there other ways that were not discussed in this chapter that travel planners might work with us to promote realistic travel expectations? Explain.

4. In your opinion, where do most of us get our ideas about desired travel destinations these days? Do you think the sources that we tend to use have changed from what they were in the past, and if yes, what are the negative and positive effects of such changes?

5. Finally, what one thing, in your opinion, contributes most to people having unrealistic expectations about travel? Explain.

Notes

_____

_____

_____

_____

_____

_____

CHAPTER 4

Increasing Trip Readiness

(or I Want to Take in Everything; No Holding Back for Me!)

By failing to prepare, you are preparing to fail.

—Benjamin Franklin

Chapter Preview

In this chapter, methods to increase our readiness and receptiveness to our upcoming travel experiences are discussed. Strategies examined include: giving us sufficient facts and practical data about travel destinations to create smooth and hassle-free travel encounters, providing us with enough background contextual information regarding our travel sites to enrich and deepen our later travel experiences, and giving us adequate opportunities for experiential learning to prime responsiveness for what is to come. Ways these strategies could be best implemented are then explored.

Using Facts and Data

In addition to deciding on our general travel objectives, we also have to make practical arrangements for our trips. This is the most common form of trip preparation for many of us. If, for instance, we are taking a big vacation trip somewhere, we know that we will need to put in place plans for things like room reservations, car rentals, and/or plane transport. We also might want to secure information about such things as driving directions to our lodgings or instructions about where to park when we arrive at our destinations. When we have all of this in order, we feel that we are, indeed, set for our upcoming journeys. But how we decide what *set* means and the degree to which we enjoy gathering this type of practical information varies across individuals.

Some of us are what might be described as data lovers (see Bare and Bare 2017). If we are high on this tendency, we like to prepare for journeys by acquiring as much advance knowledge as we can about every practical aspect of our destinations (McCrae 2004). For instance, we want to learn about the average daily temperature and weather conditions in the location we will be visiting. We look up the menus of the all the restaurants where we will be dining and calculate the driving distance from our hotel to each of those restaurants. We enjoy searching for reviews of the local golf courses where we will be playing, of all the beaches where we will be swimming, and of all the hotels where we will be staying. Our goal is to be filled with relevant data and not to be caught off guard by anything. Achieving this blissful state reassures us and gives us a sense of security.

On the other end of the spectrum, others among us are what might be called discoverers (Costa and McCrae 1988), who hate to have too many details given to us about things ahead of time. In fact, we find such advanced information searching slightly obsessive and disheartening, and believe that "knowing everything about everything" that we might encounter on our trips could actually dampen our ability to imaginatively dream about multiple trip possibilities. For us, too much pre-knowledge takes the fun out things and reduces opportunities for later trip discoveries and surprises. Of course, many of us fall somewhere in the middle on this discovery-oriented versus data-loving dimension, preferring just enough pre-trip information to help us structure and plan well for our journeys while also having enough left unknown to allow us to shift our agendas when something unscheduled unexpectedly turns out to be interesting and exciting.

We all vary considerably, therefore, on how we like to acquire and utilize pre-trip factual information. Travel planners need to be sensitive to these differences among us as they attempt to match our own information needs with the amount and type of data they provide to us. To facilitate matching our needs, it would be helpful if we were given a chance to express both *how* we prefer to get ready, in general, and *what* specifically we want to know. For instance, our travel planners might ask us questions such as: What does it take for you to feel prepared for a trip? What type of information has been made available to you on previous trips that proved to be either very helpful or unhelpful to you? How far ahead of starting your trips do you like information given to you? How much searching for facts on your own do you like to do, etc., etc.? Engaging in these sorts of discussions with a trip planner would promote finding what is just right for us in terms of our practical preparation needs, a key part of fostering positive anticipation.

Helping Us Get Ready By Creating Context

Obtaining practical information is not the only way to prepare for a trip or to build up anticipation for it. For some of us, in fact, getting ready for travel can be enhanced by being provided with contextual or background information about our destination sites to allow us to better understand and appreciate what we later see and do (see Kurtz 2017). This is particularly the case if we are high on what we call a *need for cognition* (Cacioppo and Petty 1982), or if we like to seek to understand the broader picture or the framework in which things are embedded. Frameworks help us structure and organize our perceptions and judge and evaluate our experiences. In this manner, they add coherence to what could otherwise be disparate and scattered impressions of things (Skinner and Theodossopoulos 2011).

To think about this more, imagine we had a chance to gaze at some famous stained glass windows in a Gothic cathedral in Europe. Perhaps we enjoyed looking at the windows and saw them as being beautiful, but we had no particular knowledge of any history or background relevant to what we were seeing. We did not, for instance, know the biblical stories that were being represented in each window, nor did we appreciate the complicated process ancient artisans used to produce the brilliant colors in each of the different window panes. If we had been able to acquire this type of background knowledge before our visit to this particular cathedral, it is possible that our perceptions of the windows might be very different. While gaining this kind of perspective would not guarantee us a better viewing experience, per se, it would allow us to see the windows from a very different vantage point. Context adds meaning to awareness. It can enrich experience with associations and bring appreciative awe to our perceptions.

Context, of course, can be acquired in many different ways. For instance, if we were planning a trip to New Orleans, we might be very appreciative if the hotel where we will be staying offered us beforehand links (depending on our preferences) to things like titles of fictional or non-fictional historical novels set in New Orleans and/or TV shows and movies filmed in the area. Links could also be provided to lectures given about New Orleans food or music or architectural styles or to discussions of the effects of the disastrous hurricanes that have hit the city. The list could go on and on, but the key idea is that this type of contextual preparation could provide us with a kind of *knowing* about New Orleans that could go well beyond dry, guidebook descriptions and facts. Indeed, making accessible a path to this type of contextual understanding would be like giving us a new, richer lens through which to see things more clearly and to look forward to what is to come more enthusiastically.

Experiential Priming

A third type of preparation process that can heighten our trip anticipation pleasure is less cognitive and more experiential in nature. Some of us who are strong kinesthetic learners might particularly like to prepare for our trips by being given pre-trip opportunities for more direct, hands-on experiences relevant to our upcoming journeys (Cassidy 2004). For example, if we had this type of preparation preference and we were getting ready to take our trip to New Orleans, we might love to have a chance to be exposed to some of the actual tastes and flavors of New Orleans before we set out. We might be thrilled, for instance, if the hotel where we will be staying could make available to us famous New Orleans recipes that we could directly play around with in our own kitchens before we left. This would be similar to allowing us to experience small delightful bites of something to whet our appetites prior to partaking of a banquet of delicious food. The small bites would tantalize our taste buds with *just enough* to hint at the wondrous flavors to come.

Experiential exercises, then, allow us to prepare for our journeys in ways that are sensual and direct. Besides being just fun and interesting to do, these kinds of *trying out* exercises can act as types of priming factors that enhance our readiness to perceive the world in a certain way (Henik, Friedrich and Kellog 1983). For instance, if we are primed by repeated exposure over and over to certain color words like yellow and red, we will recognize these colors faster than other colors if we are later shown them in some type of color detection task. This occurs because the primed words are still salient at some level in our consciousness (Burt 1994). Priming guides our attention and awareness in particular directions and prompts openness to certain later experiences. In this way, it facilitates responsiveness.

Questions for Discussion

Please work with the following questions to think more about how to increase travel readiness and receptivity to eventual travel encounters. Draw on your own personal experience and/or your experience in some aspect of the travel industry as you do this.

1. How would you describe your own travel preparation style in terms of your preferences for practical pre-trip information? What kind of practical information would you like travel providers (e.g., managers of the hotels where you will be staying, directors of the tours you will be participating in, etc.) to send to you before you set out on your trips? Explain.

2. Have you ever received pre-trip information packages from a travel provider that seemed especially useful and/or customized for you? If yes, please describe what was so useful about this information.

3. Besides sending practical information to us, how might travel planners work with us in other ways to increase our travel readiness? Which suggestions given in this chapter in this regard seemed most useful to you? Explain.

4. In your experience, how do most people get ready or prepare for travel? Could the travel industry do more to help make this process valuable for us in ways that go beyond the ideas presented in this chapter? Explain.

Notes

_____

_____

_____

_____

_____

_____

CHAPTER 5

Fostering Pre-Trip Excitement

(or I am So Psyched Up for This Trip I Can't Stand It!)

Your imagination is your preview of life's coming attractions.
—Albert Einstein

Chapter Preview

In this chapter, we discuss how we can use the pre-trip anticipation phase to fuel excitement for our upcoming travel. Principles of anticipation that contribute to the generation of travel enthusiasm are described, and practical strategies for implementing these principles in the trip waiting period are given. Creative ways that travel providers can work with us in this effort to make our trip anticipation experiences fun and rewarding are also explored.

Creating Excitement

As we have seen, we can use the anticipation process to foster receptivity for travel encounters. But the anticipation process can also be a fun time just in itself, and we can use it to facilitate great excitement for what is to come. We can do this by utilizing a balanced combination of holding back, drawing out, and building something up (Patel 2015). This requires constructing a disciplined pacing as we wait for an event to occur and forecasting pleasure by carefully crafting prompts related to what is to come (Roberts 2014). In this process, which is intentionally dragged out, anticipation becomes pleasurable in itself, and a sense of eagerness is created (DiPirro 2013).

As we think about this, imagine that we were planning a trip to New Mexico that was to take place in the early spring of the year. Further, imagine that we were putting together this trip in upstate New York, where the weather was still quite gray, cold, and depressing. How might we use the trip anticipation phase not just as a *getting through* period to be endured, but rather as something that sparks our enthusiasm for our trip and brings us immediate pleasure while waiting for it to start? There are many ways we might do this.

First, we could buy and pack clothes for our trip over time, rather than simply putting that off until a day or two before our journey begins. For instance, we might purchase new outfits and hiking shoes or other items which we could place in a special part of our closet to look at in anticipation of wearing them on our vacation. We might buy a pre-trip souvenir such as a small turquoise pin that we plan to wear on our plane trip to New Mexico, and then place that in a prominent place in our jewelry box to gaze at. Maybe each evening the week before our trip we could also burn special incense that has the scents of the pinon-juniper trees in it to put us in a *New Mexico mood*, or every day we could download a picture of a painting by an artist who worked in New Mexico such as Georgia O'Keefe to remind us of the beautiful landscapes and colors we will soon be witnessing firsthand. We could additionally keep a countdown calendar and, as our trip grew nearer, we could mark off each day. All of these little things would contribute to joyful looking-forward to-something experiences.

To consider more the potential power of anticipation to give joy, you might think of some memorable experiences that you have had in your lives that were enriched in some way by the anticipation process. To give some personal examples, I will relate two stories. The first involves my memories of Christmas as a child.

My mother used the art of anticipation to heighten the joy that my sister and I experienced at Christmas in our family. The buildup to Christmas was tremendous. Beautiful ornaments would be put out days ahead, and a tree would be purchased and decorated. Candles would be lit, music would be played, and the smells of evergreen and pine cones would fill the air. Drinks such as eggnog or certain cookies that we never had any other time of year would be prepared. The night before Christmas, a few very special presents would be placed under the tree, and on the morning of Christmas day, both my sister and I would awake to find a small wrapped present placed right at the foot of our beds. This was the first gift. A blow by my father on a special horn (OK, it was plastic) would signal that the day was to officially begin, and my sister and I would wait for this before we came downstairs. Then we would descend the stairs to take in the wonder and glory of all that was before us.

My mother, thus, well understood the art of anticipation. While enjoyable in themselves, these pre-event acts also set a readiness among us for what was to come. Because of this, my sister and I often ended up savoring that pre-time to Christmas as much as Christmas day itself. Clearly, the events that transpired on Christmas day could have been very similar with or without this anticipation period, but our experience of those events probably would have been much altered.

As a second example of the power of anticipation, I think of a visit my husband and I took many years ago to a museum in Bayeux, France. The point of the museum was to offer the visitor a chance to see the famous Bayeux tapestry, which is 224 feet long and was completed in the 11th century. Actually, at the time, we were not so interested in tapestries, and we only went to the museum because we could not think of anything else to do that day. What I remember most about this experience is the way the marvels of this particular tapestry were slowly revealed to us in little pieces. Visitors were led through a series of darkened hallways with beautifully lit displays. Some would show the colors in the tapestry. Some would depict various scenes. Some would show the developmental stages in making a tapestry and the incredible skill and effort it took to create these beautiful images with simple thread. By the time we got to the room where the actual tapestry was displayed, we were in a state of high excitement, and when we turned the corner and saw it in full, it was beautiful and glorious. But part of the reason we appreciated it so much was that we had spent so much time anticipating what it would be like.

We might contrast all this to another way the tapestry might have been displayed. Imagine if the museum's curators simply put the tapestry in one large room and then had a sign with an arrow pointing to this room placed in the entrance hall as one came into the museum. People then would follow this arrow and see the tapestry right away, perhaps with a placard under it telling them how many threads were involved in its making, how many hours it took to construct it, and what the scenes on it depicted. While seeing the tapestry in that situation might be of some interest to visitors, most people probably would not feel quite the same degree of joy in viewing it as they would when the buildup to its presentation was so intentionally drawn out. In fact, I have seen many tapestries since I was privileged to gaze at the Bayeux tapestry in that small museum in France, but that one remains special in my mind. Such is the power of anticipation.

Working With Travel Providers to Fuel Enthusiasm

So what can we learn from these examples of anticipation experiences? As we have seen, creating excitement in anticipation is facilitated by a combination of discipline and spontaneity, of a delaying and a prompting, and of a kind of playfulness in which we learn simply to have fun as we wait for what is to come (Kumar, Killingsworth and Gilovich 2014). Travel advisors could help us in this process by working with us to build up our excitement while we look forward to our journeys to begin. For instance, they might periodically send us reminders of how close we are to commencing our trips (e.g., "five days to go," "four days to go," etc.). They might now and then provide us with intriguing or amusing factoids about our destination places, such as "Did you know that Santa Fe was founded 10 years before the pilgrims landed?" or that "New Mexico is home to the largest hot air balloon festival in the world" (O'Donnell 2015). They might also increase our excitement by telling us about some of the fun things that other visitors to our destinations had done, or about some of the great experiences they had had.

All of this would work to fuel our enthusiasm for coming adventures and would be entertaining as well. As some have reminded us, anticipation is like having free happiness (Dunn and Norton 2014). The joy we can garner from it is only limited by the power of our imaginations. In fact, sometimes the before-the-trip phase can turn into one of the best parts of the whole trip experience, and the opportunities it offers us in this regard should not be missed.

Questions for Discussion

Please work with the following questions to think more about how to increase excitement for upcoming travel adventures. Draw on your own personal experience and/or your experience in some aspect of the travel industry as you do this.

1. As you waited for trips to begin in the past, what ways have you used to enhance your feelings of excitement about them? What was the effect of doing this? Explain.

2. Have you ever held back or deliberately dragged out how you got ready for some upcoming trip so that you could more fully savor what you eventually encountered on it (think of the Christmas and the Bayeux tapestry examples given in this chapter)? If yes, describe your experience.

3. Consider some of the suggestions given in the chapter for things you might do to increase the fun you can have as you anticipate your trips. Which of these examples were most interesting to you? Have you ever had travel advisors help you in this process? Explain.

4. What do you think prevents many people from preparing for trips in ways that are more exciting and joyful? Do you think some people are just better at this than others? Explain.

Notes

_____

_____

_____

_____

_____

_____

CHAPTER 6

Facilitating Environmental Fit I

(or Sounds Like a Great Trip for My Sister, but Not For Me!)

I wish as well as everybody else to be perfectly happy; but like everybody else, it must be in my own way.

—Jane Austen

Chapter Preview

This chapter discusses the importance to effective travel planning of finding a fit between the travel environment and one's personality styles, preferences, and value orientations. Personality styles and preferences are examined in terms of Costa and McCrae's Five-Factor Model of Personality and Plog's Psychographic Typology of Tourists. Value orientations are defined through the Values in Action approach of Petersen and Seligman.

Finding a Match

As we have seen in this book, all of us tend to feel happier and more comfortable in some types of surroundings than others. The importance to happiness of *person-environment fit*, in fact, has been the topic of much literature in psychology (Schueller 2014), where research findings have supported the simple idea that we do better and feel better in environments that match us well and bring out our strengths rather than play to our weaknesses. This is true in work settings, educational settings, and travel settings, although this latter fact is sometimes forgotten. What this means for travel is that simply providing all of us with similar dream vacations will not guarantee that we will respond to and/or enjoy these vacations in the same manner. If, for instance, we feel miserable, anxious, restless, bored, or in some other way out of tune with our circumstances, it will be hard for us to be receptive to any positive factors we encounter. However, if we are lucky enough to be placed in environments where we feel more fully at ease and in sync with our situations, our ability to savor and appreciate where we are will be enhanced. In fact, when we talk about finding wonderful travel destinations, what we often mean is simply finding situations in which our particular combination of personality styles and strengths are well suited to the travel setting we are in (Pressman, Matthews, Cohen, Martire, Scheier and Baum 2009; Rashid 2015; Diener, Larsen and Emmons 1984; Schueller 2014; Sheldon and Elliot 1999). In such environments, we are likely to experience a sense of what has been called *existential authenticity*, or a perception that we are being true to ourselves in our actions and behavior (Pearce, Filep and Ross 2011; Wang 1999). This occurs when we feel that we are not forcing things or playing fake roles, but are honestly representing ourselves as we are. Thus, pleasure in travel is a product both of what we bring to it and the qualities of the setting in which we find ourselves. Neither alone is determinative.

Let's now examine what some of the key personality dimensions are that influence our sense of fit or non-fit with our environments. We will start with an exploration of the Big Five Theory of Personality.

The Big Five

The Five-Factor Model of Personality, also known as The Big Five Theory of Personality, is what is called a trait theory of behavior. Traits are relatively stable dispositions of individuals that dispose people to behave and react in certain ways across a wide range of situations (Pervin 1989). This particular trait theory has received a great deal of attention in both the applied and theoretical research literature in psychology (Costa and McCrae 1988; John, Naumann and Soto 2008; Soni 2019). The theory proposes that there are five basic dimensions of personality on which everyone can be reliably placed: introversion/extroversion, openness, conscientiousness, agreeableness, and neuroticism. The first three have the most relevance for travel, and they will be the ones we will discuss here.

The trait of introversion/extroversion has to do with how comfortable we feel in a variety of social situations and how much arousal we tend to seek out from others in our environments. If, for example, we are high on extroversion, interactions tend to energize and build us up rather than drain or tire us. In fact, extroverts often are most edgy and bored when they are just by themselves, and they crave excitement and stimulation from the external world, especially from other people. By contrast, for those who exhibit a more introverted style, lots of social interactions tend to make us tired and fatigued. In fact, we often feel worse rather than better after such contact and yearn for some alone time to restore our energy. People who are more introverted also tend to be more cautious when in public settings than those high in extroversion and very conscious of how they think they look to others.

Openness, the second trait from the Big Five that we will describe, is related to how much we enjoy exploring unfamiliar environments and seeking out settings that are unusual and different. Those of us who are high on the trait of openness tend to be imaginative and curious and like to learn about new ideas and new perspectives. Those lower on this dimension, by contrast, are apt to be less drawn to the new and the different, and would probably be much more comfortable staying with the familiar and the tried and true.

The trait of conscientiousness relates to how responsible we tend to be in our behavior and to how important it is to be thorough and prepared for all contingencies. Those of us high on this trait tend to be reliable and careful in our behavior. By contrast, those lower on this trait often exhibit less careful and more freewheeling, spur-of-the-moment interaction styles.

The Big Five purports to assess the basic structure of personality, and numerous investigations have shown it to be predictive of our experiences in a wide range of situations, including pleasure in different types of travel environments (Jani 2014). As we think about this, it should be kept in mind that the Big Five describes general categories of behavior, and many of us fall somewhere in the middle on the represented dimensions. In fact, we probably have an intuitive sense of where we fit on these various continuums and of the affect that has on how well we manage or do not manage different types of circumstances. For instance, with regard to introversion/extroversion, we know that we can fake being more extroverted or introverted than we actually are, but that this takes great effort to do and does not feel quite right for us. The same goes for the factors of conscientiousness and openness, which orient us to the world in certain ways. Thus, these Big Five dimensions provide us with a good shortcut understanding of what kind of person we are, and, in this way, they are a very robust and useful metric to use to examine the concept of environmental fit.

Plog's Psychographic Typology of Tourists

Another interesting model to examine in terms of the concept of environmental fit in traveling is Plog's Model of Tourist Typology (Plog 1974). The model is used to categorize us into different personality types who exhibit different travel destination preferences. Although this model has had a major influence on the field of tourism studies and has been used to expand our understanding of factors that can impact an array of tourist choices and decisions, it has generated numerous critics as well as advocates among tourism researchers (see Dann 1981; Cruz-Milan 2018).

Basically, Plog (1974; 2001; 2002) suggested our travel preferences can be divided into the two dimensions of allocentric (or venturers) versus psychocentrics (or dependables). Allocentrics, similar in some ways to those high on the Big Five's dimension of openness, tend to be adventurous and curious and exhibit preferences for that which is new and novel in travel situations. Psychocentrics, on the other hand, are apt to be less adventuresome and more comfortable in familiar and structured settings where a high degree of predictability is present. Later, Plog (1991) added a dimension called energy to his model, which assesses the degree that travelers tend to be lively and vigorous versus lethargic and less energetic in their behavioral styles. All of these categories, of course, represent endpoints on continuums, just as we talked about with the Big Five, with most of us falling somewhere in the middle between the various represented poles.

While not always finding full predictive support (Litvin 2006; Smith 1990), Plog's conceptualization does seem to be getting at some core underlying factors that reliably differentiate among people who have various types of travel needs and motivations (Griffin and Albanese 1996) and who prefer different types of travel settings. Consequently, it has been a fairly durable model to explain some aspects of our travel behavior. Similar to the Big Five model, it is probably easy for most of us to say with some confidence where we fall on the allocentric/psychometric or high/low energy continuums. This conceptualization, thus, can give us a good general template to use when we are predicting the appropriateness of different types of travel venues.

Character Virtues and Strengths

In addition to looking at personality traits, a values framework can be used to predict the degree of satisfaction we might experience in different types of travel surroundings. Values are types of social cognitions that guide our ways of looking at the world and our evaluations of our own and others' behavior (Cantril and Allport 1933). They are generally more prescriptive in nature than traits; that is, they direct us to try to act in ways that might be described as being *good* or *ideal*, rather than just typical. Although there have been many conceptualizations and assessment methods utilized to define different types of values (see Rokeach 1979; Kahle 1983), a particularly interesting approach came out of a positive psychology construction. Here, instead of looking at values as abstract aspirational ideals, values are seen as virtues we all possess to a greater or lesser degree. For instance, in a model presented by Peterson and Seligman (2004), six core virtues such as wisdom and courage were identified, which encompassed 24 different character strengths, such as love of beauty or curiosity or creativity. These character strengths, empirically derived from self-reports of our actual behavior in different situations, are hypothesized to paint pictures of our functioning at its very best. In such circumstances, we feel *on top of our game* and highly energized and fully alive. We are, in a word, flourishing (Govindji and Linley 2007; Sheldon and Elliot 1999; Seligman 2012).

As can be seen, in this strength-based approach, the focus of inquiry is shifted. Rather than directly assessing general traits, it asks us to empirically describe situations in which we feel effective and invigorated, and then character strengths and patterns of virtues are inferred from that. For instance, we may come to recognize that we feel best in situations where we are given the opportunity to be creative or to express our love for learning or to exhibit our natural social intelligence. Whatever our particular strengths are, when we express them we feel a lack of strain and a deep sense of rightness, which is both energizing and restoring.

The Three Models

These three models offer us different perspectives on what it means to describe oneself as a person. Each model shines a light on us in a slightly different way, so travel providers have a choice about how to utilize them in ways that best suit our particular needs. We will explore more about this in the next chapter.

Questions for Discussion

Before we turn to the next chapter, though, please work with the following questions to think more about the importance of finding a fit between your personality traits and styles and the travel environment in which you are in. Draw on your own personal experience and/or your experience in some aspect of the travel industry as you do this.

1. How would you describe your travel personality style? What are your key strengths? Have you ever been in a travel environment in which your styles and strengths were particularly well-matched and/or not well-matched? Explain.

2. Do you think travel venues on typical tour packages tend to privilege or favor some personality types more than others? If yes, explain. What has been your own experience with this?

3. Existential authenticity is the perception that one is being very true to oneself in one's particular environmental situation. Have you ever had this experience of authenticity on some trip that you were tak-

ing, or have you seen it occur among others? If yes, what facilitated this?

4. Try to describe your perfect travel setting in terms of some of the dimensions discussed in this chapter. What kinds of places would you visit? Where would you stay? How would you use your time? Which of your strengths would be brought out?

Notes

_____

_____

_____

_____

_____

_____

Notes

CHAPTER 7

Facilitating Environmental Fit II

(or Do Those Psychological Tests Really Tell Us Anything?)

I want freedom for the full expression of my personality.
—Mahatma Gandhi

Chapter Preview

In Chapter 6 models of personality and value preferences that predict travel satisfaction or dissatisfaction in different situations were discussed. This chapter examines the important applied question of how data based on these models can be best gathered and utilized by travel providers to enhance travel well-being.

Direct Collection of Personality Information

Theoretical models of personality can be conceptually interesting to consider, but travel providers need ways of securing actual data based on them to make such models practically useful. One way to collect information relevant to our personalities and styles is to simply gather such data directly from us. Various short and long forms are available for each of the assessment approaches discussed in the previous chapter.

For instance, Costa and McCrae's Big Five Dimensions can be measured using 50 to 60-item inventories (Srivastava 2021) or an abbreviated 10-item assessment form (Rammstedt and John 2007). Plog's allocentric/

psychocentric categories can be determined using a brief five-item scale (Plog 1974) or a 10-item version that includes the dimension of traveler energy (Plog 1991). Assessment tools are also available that measure 28 personality factors identified by Plog as co-varying with allocentric and psychocentric tendencies, and that assess travelers' endorsement of vacation scenarios that are described as being either allocentric or psychocentric in nature (Griffith and Albanese 1996). Finally, the Values in Action (VIA) characteristics described by Peterson and Seligman (2004) can be determined either by the use of the original 240-item scale or a 24-item short form (McGrath and Wallace 2021).

Thus, many options exist for assessing our basic personality styles, travel destination preferences, and value orientations. To facilitate discussions about optimal travel choices, travel planners might have us complete either one or several of these scales before we embark on our journeys. They could then go over the results with us and use them as a springboard for discussions about how different types of travel venues and agendas would or would not be a good match for our patterns of strengths and traits.

The Big Data Approach

Another way to gather personality profile information is more indirect and would entail the utilization of so-called Big Data. Big Data refers to the enormous amount of information that can be gathered from analyses of our digital footprints from such things as Google searches, Facebook postings, mobile phone locations, and so forth. This type of data has long been used to assess consumer preferences and probable future buying likes and dislikes (Wedel and Kannan 2016). What is newly emerging, however, is the potential for analyzing and mining these types of Big Data sources not just to secure information about what kind of products we tend to like or to dislike, but also to provide pictures of what type of people we are. Many analysts in the field, in fact, are now suggesting that Big Data can increasingly provide a window on our basic attitudes, strengths, personality styles, and emotional tendencies (Matz and Netzer 2017). The ability to infer this type of information from digital data sources has big implications for the travel industry because, as we have

seen, our built-in psychological predispositions and traits have a significant influence on our satisfaction or dissatisfaction with various types of
travel environments (Kosinski, Stillwell and Graepel 2013).

Of course, with the passing of policy guidelines such as the General
Data Protection Regulation (GDPR) in the European Union in 2016,
organizations are becoming more careful about how they handle such
data. The GDPR regulates how information derived from various forms
of analytic procedures can be collected and utilized in ways that protect
the privacy of the consumer (Terra 2020). This means that data collected
from these types of Big Data digital records have to be used in a manner
that is sufficiently sensitive to our rights. At the very least, we would
have to be alerted that such data has been gathered, and we would have to
give our permission to have it applied in different ways. As with so much
else that we have discussed in this book, this means that a collaborative
effort between our travel providers and us would be required to ensure
that any Big Data that is collected on us is used only in a manner that
supports our best interests.

With this in mind, we will now turn to a hypothetical narrative about
two travelers that will highlight some of the practical possibilities for
using information about a traveler's personality and values to inform a
variety of hospitality decisions. Although this is a hypothetical tale, it
shows some of the options hospitality staff have to creatively use different
types of data to enhance their clients' travel experiences.

A Tale of Two Travelers

Picture two individuals whom we will name Sean and Marianne, who
are staying in the same hotel in a city somewhere in the United States.
Imagine that the management of their hotel either had access to so-called
Big Data digital footprints for both these individuals, or they had copies
of personality and value assessments that these two individuals filled out
themselves and gave permission to the hotel staff to look at. Imagine further that after the management conducted an initial review of these data,
they concluded that both Sean and Marianne would probably be high
on what we have identified as an allocentric travel style (they like what is
new and novel), but they added the important caveat that both of these

travelers would most likely be different in terms of how they would prefer their specific allocentric goals to be met.

In this tale, our managers then decided to go back to their data to see what further patterns might emerge from it. From these analyses, they predicted that in addition to allocentrism, Sean would probably be rather high on the traits of introversion and conscientiousness and would likely feel energized if he could exhibit his core strength of love of learning. Thus, they expected that although he may want to find exciting and challenging adventures on his trip: (1) he probably would not like being in big social gatherings, (2) he would tend to be self-conscious in public settings, (3) he would probably value certainty and pre-planning of activities well ahead of time as opposed to just letting things remain loose and unscheduled, and (4) he would be apt to love situations where he felt he could either teach or learn some new knowledge from others. Further, through the examination of Sean's responses to an in-house general interest survey that he completed, the hotel managers also knew that Sean particularly likes sports activities such as swimming and hiking, enjoys touring historical sites and exploring old ruins, and loves playing string instruments such as the violin or guitar or mandolin.

Now let's suppose that the managements' re-analyses of Marianne's digital records yielded a very different picture of her, and that the management surmised very different things about her. First, although Marianne, too, was assumed to like new and novel travel situations, they correctly judged that she would be a rather extroverted, spur-of-the-moment type person who seemed to have a special strength of high social intelligence. Thus, the managers inferred that unlike Sean, she would: (1) probably love big social gatherings and chances to meet lots of new people on her trip, (2) be low on self-consciousness in public settings, (3) not be especially fond of too much pre-planning of events, and (4) very much like to participate in spontaneously put together activities in which physical strength and social astuteness are required. From her interest survey, the management also determined that Marianne particularly likes sports such as hang gliding, race car driving, and volleyball.

With this sort of data available, very customized *just-for-you* information packets could be created for both our hypothetical travelers. For instance, because the hotel management knew that Sean enjoys touring historical sites but does not like big social outings, special information about privately guided tours of famous sites in the vicinity of the hotel could be provided to him in advance of his arrival. Because the management further knew that Sean enjoys swimming and hiking if they can be carried out in rather solitary ways, they might guess that he would be appreciative of descriptions of quiet, adult swim hours at the hotel pool, or in receiving maps of self-directed hiking trails in the area. To further personalize Sean's services, the staff at his hotel could also offer to directly connect him to people and resources in the community, which allow him to enhance and build on his unique areas of interest and learn about new things. For example, hotel managers might provide Sean with the name of local string musicians in the area and give him the dates for local concerts and other musical performances going on in the community during the time of his stay.

For Marianne a different type of suggested itinerary might be offered to her. Because the hotel management knew that she enjoys chances to socialize with others and meet new people and also has an interest in volleyball, she could be given information about a schedule for pick- up volleyball games that take place daily at a sports facility near the hotel. The managers also might provide Marianne with the times for the social hour at the hotel bar where drinks are priced at two-for-one and people get a chance to intermingle and chat while live music is playing in the background. She additionally could be given names of individuals in the community who have interests in car racing and those who offer classes in hang gliding, which is one of her special passions.

Coming Back to Finding a Fit

Although the preceding story about the two travelers is hypothetical, the point is that very specific user profiles could be created that would enable people in the hospitality industry to provide experiences that are tailored to us, and that could be used in subsequent guest loyalty programs to build even more customized services (ReviewPro 2019).

Environments, in general, could also be structured to fit our different needs and styles in other ways. To give just a few examples considering the trait of introversion/extroversion, opportunities for interactions in different types of travel environments could be created where we could be either social or alone, depending on our preferences. Cruise ships, for instance, might offer a choice of both communal and private two-person tables in their restaurants, and tours in various ports of call could include group- and self-led options. Recreational possibilities on board cruise liners could range from public games to in-room broadcasts of shipboard performances, and half-price happy hour drink specials could be provided at certain hours both in energetic bar settings and as room service delivery options, and so on.

The actual physical design of hotels and resorts could also be made to accommodate different tastes and preferences. For instance, resort hotels might offer options for both private in-room whirlpool bathing and access to more communal outdoor hot tubs. Traditional inns might feature quiet reading and meditation rooms in addition to social gathering spaces in lobbies. Tours might even be marketed in terms of their suitability for those of us who exhibit different personality styles or destination preferences or patterns of virtues. By offering this sort of flexibility, trip planners and others in the travel industry could work with us to provide travel opportunities that bring out our best and that change trips that might have ended up being rather unremarkable or wrong in some way into ones that are memorable and especially rewarding.

Questions for Discussion

Please work with the following questions to think more about how different types of data can be obtained and utilized to customize travel experiences and enhance levels of travel satisfaction. Draw on your own personal experience and/or your experience in some aspect of the travel industry as you do this.

1. Would knowledge that your travel providers had access to your digital data footprints make you happy or concerned? Explain. Do you think access to this kind of customer Big Data by those in the travel industry would be likely to make traveling more or less enjoyable for most of us? Explain.

2. We have talked about how travel providers might also use data collected from direct personality assessments to better customize our travel services and experiences. Would you like this sort of option made available to you in your own travels? Why or why not? Can you think of any downsides to these sorts of service customization efforts? Explain.

3. As was briefly explored in this chapter, in addition to being physical travel destinations, more and more hotels are also serving as types of conduits or brokers for their guests to access resources and experiences in the local community. Have you had any experience with this? How might this trend change how we define good and bad travel experiences?

4. What particular idea or ideas about how to create different types of physical spaces for those of us who exhibit different personality styles and/or value preferences stood out to you the most? Explain. Have you ever been in a travel environment in which this type of flexibility was offered to guests?

Notes

_____

_____

_____

_____

_____

_____

Case Study 1:
Pre-trip Anticipation

You have read about the nature of travel anticipation and the elements involved in making this anticipation period useful and joyful. Now here is a chance to apply the ideas presented on this topic to a hypothetical travel case study. Doing this will allow you to more actively work with the concepts discussed in Part I of the book and to integrate them to solve real-life types of travel dilemmas. There are no right or wrong answers, so do not be held back by searching for the so-called correct solution. Just try to draw on your own experiences and on the frameworks that were provided to try to critically analyze the presented case.

The Story of Katy

Imagine that a person we will call Katy just won a one-week, all expenses paid trip to Paris. Katy is very excited because all of her life she wanted to travel to France. From the pictures she has seen of Paris, she has decided that it must be the most beautiful city in the world, and that the people who live and work there must be incredibly happy most of the time. Katy loves all things French, including French food and wine, French literature, and even the sound of the French language. She describes herself as a *crazy* kind person who enjoys being around other people and having fun. Now Katy is in a tizzy about how to best prepare for her trip. As part of her prize, all practical arrangements for her trip have been made and paid for (e.g., plane tickets were purchased, hotel reservations were made, etc.), but Katy wants to get ready in other ways, as well. In her own jargon, she wants to *get really psyched up* for this trip and prepare for it in a manner that should yield the most positive outcomes for her.

It is your job as the head of the contest that Katy won to work with Katy to help get her ready for her journey in such a way as to increase the likelihood that her travel experiences will be positive and satisfactory. You have three weeks to assist Katy in getting ready.

Brainstorm how you would work with Katy during her three-week trip preparation period. What kinds of advice would you give her? What types of resources and information might you make available to her? What type of data might you collect from her? What questions would you ask her? What would you tell her to definitely do or not do as she waits for her trip to Paris to commence? Try to be as creative as you can here and to consider all the ways that you might work collaboratively with Katy to help ensure that she is, indeed, ready and open for what could potentially be a wonderful dream trip.

Notes

_____

_____

_____

_____

_____

_____

PART II

The Actual Trip

Jobs fill your pocket, but adventures fill your soul.
—Jaime Lyn Beatty

We have seen how part of the joy of traveling can consist of relishing the anticipation of a trip before it occurs. This anticipation can assist us in setting up frameworks and mindsets to allow us to better enjoy our later actual travel experiences. But anticipation and getting ready are only part of the travel process. In this part of the book, we talk about how people in the travel industry can help us find joy during our actual trips and what obstacles might have to be addressed to facilitate this.

CHAPTER 8

Ameliorating Travel Fatigue

(or I Am So Tired and Stressed I Don't Care How Beautiful the Ocean Is!)

Jet lag is for amateurs.
—Dick Clark

Chapter Preview

The powerful negative effects that fatigue, stress, and exhaustion can play on our ability to achieve travel satisfaction are discussed in this chapter. Remedies are examined that can help ameliorate both short-term, travel-related conditions such as jet lag or temporary sleep deprivation and more general, long-term feelings of lack of well-being. As part of this examination, a brief description of the health and wellness travel movement is included, as well as an overview of what it means to deeply savor something.

Travel Fatigue

One major obstacle we can encounter when we embark on trips is the simple fact that traveling today can be quite tiring and just plain hard. This is true of both the setbacks we can face while traveling on route to our destinations and the difficulties we can encounter at our destinations themselves. All of this can be overlooked in the utopia of planning a trip and thinking about how wonderful it all will be. We ponder our upcoming vacations and imagine that we will continuously experience peace, quiet, and deep relaxation or exciting fun (Kurtz 2017). But traveling, as we all know, can involve many physical, mental, and emotional hassles, and these hassles can sometimes sap energy and turn what we had expected to be a restful journey into an exhausting challenge to endure.

Imagine, for instance, that we are embarking on a trip to some faraway Caribbean island. As we think of this trip, we see ourselves swimming in lovely aqua blue water or lying sunbathing on white sand with the scent of tropical flowers and the sound of the surf gently lulling us to sleep. Ah... wonderful. But the reality might be quite different. First, we have to get to the island of our dreams in order to enjoy it. This may involve getting out of bed in the wee hours of the night, driving in heavy traffic to an airport, encountering difficulty in finding a parking spot there, lugging heavy bags up and down curbs, waiting in long lines for check-in and security, putting up with airline schedule delays, sitting in a plane for hours in a small and uncomfortable seat, eating strange-tasting food on the plane during a time that is off our usual eating schedule, transferring at some point to another even smaller and more uncomfortable plane for the final leg of the journey, and then renting a car in a culture that is new to us. So when we finally arrive at our hotel, we are not feeling ecstatic but rather just tired and grumpy. Even though our room may be beautiful, the bed is different from the one we have at home, and the light comes into our room in the morning earlier than we are used to. Thus, our sleep patterns are disrupted. We additionally can end up eating all kinds of food that we normally avoid, and this can wreak havoc with our digestive system. We may also be suffering from jet lag or sleep deprivation caused by taking early red-eye flights that make us feel weak and slightly disoriented. Finally, even after we have adjusted to our new sleeping and eating schedules, we may still feel stressed from having to expend a lot of energy negotiating a new milieu with which we are not completely familiar. All of this is quite taxing.

Helping Us Deal With Short-Term Travel Fatigue

The above is not to say that there are not wonderful aspects to traveling, but simply to suggest that many parts of it can pose difficulties for us that diminish our well-being. Although these difficulties can't be simply wiped away, there are things that people in the travel industry could put in place to lessen the impact of some of them.

To start with, as we talked about earlier in the book, a travel planner could work with us to assist us in organizing trips that were not over-scheduled or involved too much strenuous traveling from one location to another. For instance, on a one-week trip to Europe, it would be more reasonable for us to try to visit only two or three major cities rather than touring a different city each day. We might also be advised not to cram too many events into our daily touring outings and to be sure to insert rest periods or downtimes into our travel agendas. All of these things could work to ameliorate the fatigue that comes from having unworkable travel goals. Travel planners could also help us book flights or arrange other modes of transportation that, to the extent possible, did not involve many tiring connections and long stopovers between different legs of our journeys.

After we arrive at our destinations, travel providers there could additionally work with us to help us recuperate from other types of travel hassles. For instance, for the very jet-lagged among us, hotel staff might have flexible check-in times that allow us to access our rooms on schedules that fit our own internal clocks rather than the official time at our destination places. Staff also could extend hours for serving us meals like breakfast when we first arrive and/or make available to us light, healthy food that helps with jet lag syndromes (Fletcher 2020). To increase our comfort, discounts could additionally be offered to us for various restorative guest services such as in-room massage or aromatherapy.

Other sorts of short-term restorative situations could be created for those of us who simply need a way to recharge from the rigors of days spent touring. For example, a hotel that had a beautiful garden in the back of its property could make revitalizing garden walks available to us in which the scent of flowers, the visual beauty of plants, and the sound of waterfalls produce calming feelings. Or, for those of us who prefer more direct tactile sensations, *refresh packages* could be offered that include things like gentle stretching activities or soothing soaks in warm tubs filled with calming oils. The point is that environments could be structured that allow us to become revitalized in ways that best suit us.

Wellness Vacations: Promoting Revitalization

While some of us just want to recover from short-term travel fatigue or restore ourselves now and then from everyday travel hassles, for others the whole point of taking our trips is to enhance our general sense of well-being. Wellness resorts and spas have been around for a long time in many different cultures, but they are surging in popularity again today (Koncul 2012). In part, this popularity reflects a more inclusive way of looking at the nature of positive functioning (Bickenbach 2017) that differentiates between wellness as being simply a lack of disease versus a definition that emphasizes a broader wholeness and balance in body, mind, and spirit. *Health*, in this latter conceptualization, is not seen as being a neutral state in which illness is not present, but rather a condition in which we flourish in multiple spheres of our lives (Mueller and Kaufman 2000).

To meet the increasing interest in this kind of wellness, a wide spectrum of services are now available, including offerings that cater to those of us in different life stages who have different sorts of needs and preferences (Smith and Puczko 2009). For instance, activities in *health tourism* facilities can include services to enhance the wellness of our spirits (yoga, meditation, chanting), our physical bodies (massage, healing waters, physical fitness training, saunas, mud baths), and our minds (lectures, inspirational readings, group discussions). There are also resorts that offer simple pampering, or what might be called sanctuary environments for us (Stephens 2020). We can find hotels that include amenities such as private plunge pools and lanais, personal chefs, and in-room massage and beauty treatments. The choices that are available are endless in this regard, and all such services work to restore our sense of vitality and wholeness. However, to benefit maximally from them, we have to be able to savor what is offered to us. We will turn to a discussion of the idea of savoring next.

Thinking More About Savoring

Savoring entails a heightening of pleasure in something by intentionally directing awareness to it. In this sense, it is a type of mindfulness, but a kind of mindfulness in which we deliberately focus on positive, not neutral or negative events (Dube and Le Bel 2001). Savoring draws out and elongates pleasure. It involves an appreciative receptivity to the good and beauty around one (Bryant and Veroff 2007). Although savoring does not necessarily have to be accompanied by a slowing down of our behavior (we can savor fleeting instances), slowness does often add to our ability to pay attention to what is before us in a more thoughtful way than if we were more hurried or rushed in our activities (see Shulman 1992).

To think more about this idea of savoring, we might imagine what this kind of state, in fact, feels like. When we do this, we should notice that savoring is multifaceted and involves input from divergent sensory modalities, including sights, sounds, smells, and touch (Le Bel and Dube 2001; Kringelbach and Berridge 2010).

Let's say that we were sunbathing on the beach sometime during our vacation after a tiring afternoon of museum touring the day before. As we feel the warmth of the sun on our skin, we can also intentionally attend to other sensations that would deepen our experience. For instance, we might bring into our awareness the sound of sea birds or children playing; we might take in the smell of the salt sea air; we might listen to the rhythm of the waves as they rise and then retreat on the beach, and attend to the small space between these patterns when there is a certain magical stillness. Learning to relax in a savoring manner means learning how to wallow in and soak up delight from multiple sensations that we bring into our focus as we respond to something. When we bring this kind of awareness to our situation, we say we are luxuriating in our experience. In such a state, we are simply receptive to our surroundings, not acting on them, and we are restored in a deep and satisfying way.

Of course, environments exist even in very expensive luxury hotels that are not particularly conducive to savoring. Distractions, noise, and jarring sounds impede savoring experiences. Loud colors, crowded settings, and uncomfortable climates make achieving this state less feasible. For some, a very public setting is less amenable to this sort of letting go and wallowing than more private arrangements, while for others, the public/private distinction is less important.

The above suggests all wellness settings are not created alike. What might cause one of us to delight in a particular experience and come away feeling very refreshed and satisfied may not work as well for another. Relaxation and savoring, in general, do not always come easily to many of us, and a little extra attention and thoughtful care on the part of travel providers to find situations that are particularly suited to us would be well worth the effort it might take. Experiencing savoring relaxation is the framework that allows us to dive into our later trip experiences with full zest and energy, an outcome that increases our ability to appreciate what we encounter.

Questions for Discussion

Please work with the following questions to think more about the problems of travel fatigue and the nature of wellness, and about how travel providers might work with us to reduce the former and enhance the latter. Draw both on your personal experiences as a traveler and/or any experiences you have had in the travel industry as you do this.

1. What has helped you most to get over jet lag or fatigue from tiring flights or other modes of travel on trips that you have taken? Have you ever used any *restorative services* or techniques similar to the ones mentioned in this chapter? If yes, describe.
2. What suggestion or suggestions made in this chapter about how to promote recovery from short-term travel fatigue were most interesting to you? Explain. Are there other things that were not mentioned that you would like people in the travel industry to make available to promote short-term relaxation and restoration from tiring trips?
3. Have you ever gone on a spa or wellness vacation similar to the ones described in this chapter, or known someone who went on such a trip? If yes, please describe and talk about what you or they liked best and least about it.
4. Consider now the concept of savoring. Many of us have difficulty savoring or relaxing easily. Why do you think this is so? Are most of the travel environments you have been in (e.g., hotels, airports and other transportation centers, restaurants, etc.) relaxing places that are conducive to savoring? If no, how could this be improved?

Notes

_____

_____

_____

_____

_____

_____

CHAPTER 9

Mitigating Comparison Tendencies

(or I Was Happy Here Until I Saw <u>Your</u> Room!)

Comparison doesn't strengthen anything other than your own insecurities.

—AC Dyson

Chapter Preview

In this chapter, the damaging effects that negative comparisons to others can have on travel satisfaction are discussed. These types of comparisons are often so harmful because they can generate in us deep feelings of unfairness. The dynamics of this are explored, and communication strategies those in the travel industry can use to help us feel less of a need to make damaging comparisons are examined.

The Insidiousness of Comparisons

In addition to physical hassles, traveling can also involve a lot of negative social comparisons. This is because traveling takes us out of our normal routines and predictable environments and makes us prone to look to others to give ourselves a benchmark of what we should have and do (Nawijn, Marchand, Veenhoven and Vingerhoets 2010). These comparisons with others, as we discussed previously, can sometimes occur in the pre-trip traveling stage. However, they can also occur during our actual trips and have several detrimental effects (Collins 1996). To give a few examples, let's imagine that we just checked onto a cruise ship, and we perceive that others are getting better deals than we are in terms of things like room sizes or amenity packages. Or maybe we observe that our service at a restaurant seems to be slower than that given to people sitting at the table next to us, or that our glasses of wine are smaller than theirs. These types of comparisons can go on and on and can be insidious and deflating. They occur most frequently when our notions of what we think we deserve are unclear, and when we are not sure of what is our due. Consequently, we look to others for information about what is the norm. Interestingly, psychological research has shown that the more we compare our lot with others, especially if the comparisons are negative, the unhappier and more miserable we become (Wheeler and Miyake 1992). This is the case because when we continually compare ourselves with someone else, we basically allow what happens to them and not to us to determine our own happiness.

As a personal example related to this, I recall a situation when my husband and I stayed some years ago in a small hotel in Europe. Initially, when we viewed our assigned room at this hotel, we were quite pleased with it. Even though the walls were a bit dingy and the rug a bit worn, the room seemed quiet and comfortable and a good place to relax and settle in. We had an excellent night's sleep and woke up the next morning hungry and ready to go to breakfast. Unfortunately, though, as we were walking to the breakfast area, we noticed that the door to the room next to us happened to be left open, and we decided to peek inside. What we saw when we did this was a beautifully appointed space. Walls were freshly painted, drapes appeared new, and the floor was highly polished. Suddenly our *comfortable* room seemed rather shabby. We were confused at this point, so we went down to the hotel lobby to ask the desk clerk if the nicely decorated rooms were much more expensive than our room, but he said there was no price difference. He also rather dismissively explained that the hotel was in the process of renovating all of its rooms and that only about half of them had been finished. Then when we requested to be moved to a nice room, he curtly informed us that all of the nice rooms were already booked so such a switch was impossible! We, of course, became very upset, and this incident turned what had started out as a very pleasant experience at this hotel into something we fumed about for a long time. The word we used most often to describe our situation was unfair. Let's think more about this concept of unfairness, and why it is so important to us.

Comparisons and Unfairness Assessments

Perceptions of unfair outcomes are powerful igniters of dissatisfaction, and they occur most often when we think that we did not get what we rightly earned in some situation (Walster, Walster and Bersheid 1978). For instance, if we paid what we thought was a great amount of money for a very nice hotel room and then were given only a rather plain room overlooking the back alley, we would be more upset than if we paid a small amount of money for this same room. This is the case because in the former situation, we would have felt that we deserved a good room more than in the latter case.

We also can perceive other kinds of situations to be unfair that have less to do with the specific outcomes we receive. For instance, we can define situations to be unfair if we think we have not been treated with the degree of dignity and respect that we feel is our due (Mikula, Petri and Tanzer 1990). As an example of this, imagine a case in which we were asking a question to a hotel clerk about directions to a place we wanted to visit only to have the clerk answer us very briefly and dismissively and then move on to dealing with someone else. Even though in the scheme of things this is a small event, interactions of this kind can trigger powerful emotions because they can make us feel discounted and unimportant.

To think about this more, we can go back to the incident in the small hotel in Europe that was described earlier where my husband and I were given a shabby room compared to others, and then were treated rudely by the hotel clerk when we later asked about this. This incident, as I noted, was very upsetting to us. As my husband and I considered why it was so disturbing, we realized that it would have been helpful if, when we were initially checking in, we had been told that some of the rooms were updated and some were not, and that only non-updated rooms were available now. At that point, we could have made a decision whether to stay in that hotel or not. It would also have been helpful if it was explained to us how decisions about being given the updated rooms had been made in the first place. Maybe, for instance, people had to make reservations for these nice rooms considerably in advance, or maybe they were being saved for longtime repeat patrons of the hotel who were enrolled in different kinds of loyalty programs. It would not have mattered so much what the rules were, just that the rules were explicitly described to us, and that we could make decisions about what to do in light of those rules.

In the preceding example, openness and directness of communication were sorely lacking, and this led to very bad feelings on the part of my husband and me. When openness and directness of communication are present, by contrast, feelings of resentment are reduced because the vague misunderstandings that often fuel irritation are eliminated. This is key. It is uncertainty and lack of clarity that tend to lead us to the uninformed comparisons that can spark anger (Collins 1996). Open and direct communication is accessible, responsive, and transparent (CSPonline 2016). This means that communication is enhanced when we can contact our travel providers easily when we have needs, when the providers are able to quickly respond to our requests and questions, and when reasons for making different types of travel decisions for us are made clear. Let's talk about this more and look at how people in the travel industry can facilitate this kind of communication.

Enhancing Good Communication Patterns

One change that has been evident in travel today, as well as in society as a whole, is the increasing use of technology to communicate with others. Because of all the advances in such technology, travel providers have more and more opportunities to engage in accessible and open communication with us than ever before (Shashou 2017).

As an example of this, imagine that we were staying in some typical hotel where we had a question about hotel policies or the use of amenities, and we wanted to talk with someone on the hotel staff about our concerns. Perhaps, for instance, we saw other hotel guests heading out on bicycle rides or paddling in kayaks on a lake behind the hotel, and we wondered why we were not told about these possibilities. Or maybe we called down to the hotel restaurant at 5 PM to make a reservation for dinner that evening only to be told that we needed to make reservations by

4 PM in order to get a table. Whatever our particular concerns, it would be helpful if we could have them addressed quickly before confusion and irritation set in. This is where technology is useful. In addition to trying to seek out chances for in-person interactions with hotel employees when we have questions, at many hotels these days we can also consult with staff remotely through the use of apps available on our smartphones or iPads or other similar devices (Shashou 2017). This adds efficiency to the process of getting answers back to us. Some hotels additionally offer access to things like virtual concierges online where frequently asked questions are responded to (What You Should Know 2019), or in-room kiosks where we can make service requests on our own schedules and at our own convenience without leaving our rooms or picking up a phone (Adler and Gordon 2013). Visual information regarding hotel amenities such as pictures of the hotel restaurant's interior or gym facilities is also increasingly being made available via different types of media to give us better ideas of options from which we can choose. Many hotels, in fact, have large touch screens in place in lobbies (Adler and Gordon 2013) that we can use for this purpose. Other establishments utilize things like photo framing applications to depict what is going on in different places in the hotel at any given moment (Chiasson 2010). For example, current events and gatherings at the hotel might be highlighted, restaurant specials noted and pictured, loyalty programs explained, or where to purchase ongoing tour tickets described. Access to these types of communication sources would enable us to make more informed decisions about how to best structure and use our time. This would give us a greater sense that we are in control of the communication process, a feeling that is very empowering.

The above represents just a few of the possibilities that new technology offers us to enhance our quality of communication in travel situations. Of course, direct in-person consultations with travel staff might be the preferred mode of interaction for some of us, and that could be used when appropriate. The important idea is that we should be given expanded options for the use of multiple and easily accessible communication channels so that our questions and requests can be quickly addressed. This would cause us to rely less on uninformed or misleading sources to gather information, an outcome that can generate the resentment and dissatisfaction that we all want to avoid!

Questions for Discussion

Please work with the following questions to think more about the impact that negative comparisons with others can have on travel satisfaction and how this could be best dealt with by those in the travel industry. Draw on your own personal experience and/or your experiences in some aspect of the travel industry as you do this.

1. Think of a time on a trip that you took when you compared yourself to some other traveler in some way and ended up feeling less satisfied with your own situation as a result. Describe the scene and try to analyze it in terms of the ideas about comparisons presented in this chapter.

2. Now consider a time on a vacation when you were not just upset by some incident that occurred, but you also thought you had been treated very unfairly by someone in the hospitality industry. Again, describe the scene and try to frame your answer by using the concepts about unfairness and deservingness presented in this chapter.

3. Turn now to an examination of the idea of the importance of treating others with respect. How would you define the concept of respect? Give an example of how a person in the travel industry might treat you: (1) disrespectfully, and then (2) respectfully. What is the key difference?

4. Good communication includes the qualities of openness, transparency, and accessibility. Give a description of how a hotel check-in clerk would act if he or she either valued or did not value these three aspects of good communication. Which strategies offered in this chapter to enhance these dimensions of communication were most interesting to you? Explain.

5. Using different forms of technology to enhance our access to information and advice during our travels was also considered in this chapter. Have you ever had any personal experience with this? Do you think technology will have a positive impact on the ways we interact with people in the hospitality industry? Explain.

Notes

_____

_____

_____

_____

_____

_____

CHAPTER 10

Reducing Travel Habituation I

(or I Used to Love These Kinds of Hotels, but Now They Seem a Little Ho-Hum to Me!)

Boredom is the deadliest poison.

—William F. Buckley Jr.

Chapter Preview

In this chapter, the problem of non-responsiveness to our surroundings is discussed using the concepts of habituation and anchor shifting. Habituation occurs when we become less interested in something due to repeated exposure to it, and anchor shifting occurs when a change of standards for making comparisons takes place. Both can cause us to be less impressed by and receptive to situations that previously pleased us. One remedy that travel providers can use to mitigate habituation is to allow us to personalize or put on our unique stamp on our travel spaces. The ways that this can be implemented are discussed.

Nothing Excites Us Anymore

We live in a time in which we can choose among more travel options than ever before. For instance, we can go on safari vacations, work-with-the-locals trips, outdoor adventure outings, and/or on spa wellness tours, to name just a few. While this richness of offerings is a positive development, so much choice can also make us feel a bit weary and burned out, and we can begin to sense that we have just done and seen it all. Below we will take a deeper look at some of the things that produce these ho-hum dynamics in traveling, and then examine how these feelings can be reduced by strategies employed by those in the travel industry.

Anchoring Issues

Let's start by turning once again to an examination of the importance to our happiness of the kinds of comparisons that we make. As we have seen, we are comparative in nature, and we use feedback from others to judge the merit of our own experiences (Festinger 1954). We also use feedback about our own past encounters to evaluate our present circumstances (Larsen and McKibban 2008), and this can also impact our enjoyment of the present. For instance, if we see a truly spectacular ballet performance by the visiting Bolsoi Ballet, we may become less enthusiastic the next day when we go to see our local college ballet recital that we had previously loved to attend. This is because our anchor for judgment was reset by seeing the best performers in the world. What was once considered excellent now became subpar (Gilbert 2007). Ironically, this means that the ante for finding joy in the present is continually upped with the more exposure we have had in the past to that which is truly first-rate and special.

Habituation

Another way that we can become burned out in travel is simply by repeated exposure to things. This has to do with the phenomena of habituation that is the bane of the seasoned traveler (and the travel industry!). The fact is that we often grow bored with familiar things that we have seen again and again (Frederick and Loewenstein 1999). Although for some of us, routine and predictability are soothing and satisfying, for many it simply creates over time a kind of mindlessness or dulling of our responses to our environment.

I think here of a friend who was lucky enough to become a famous actor in a popular TV series. When he traveled after his show became a hit, he always went first class. Usually, because of his fame, flowers and fruit baskets would be left in his hotel room for him to enjoy, and special perks such as free drinks or snacks would be provided to him. At first, he was very excited and appreciative of all of this extra attention, but over time he grew so used to it that he hardly noticed it anymore. In fact, when my husband and I traveled with him, he would often give us the fruit and flowers to take back to our much humbler accommodations.

This little story represents the dilemma we often face in life. We both thrive on change and yet draw comfort from predictability. The key is to get the balance right between the two.

Helping Travelers Reduce Ho-Hum *Been There* Feelings

What this suggests in practical terms is that for many of us to be fully appreciative and receptive to where we are, we have to be just a bit jolted out of our *automatic pilot* way of being. Often to enhance our responsiveness to something, we need some kind of change in our environment or something new to draw our attention. We have to learn to see again and, in a sense, be awakened or re-awakened to our surroundings.

To think more about this, imagine an individual who travels a lot, who has increasingly become aware that different types of commercial travel lodgings are all beginning to look alike. Perhaps after a while, this traveler desperately wants something different. The increased popularity of homestays and other travel accommodations in private dwellings, in fact, attests to the idea that this traveler is not alone in her feelings. What many of us are looking for as we travel nowadays is not always simple convenience or comfortable sameness, but something more remarkable, interesting, and memorable (Pine and Gilmore 2019). But how can we find these remarkable experiences, and what can those in the travel industry do to help us in this process?

Personalizing Our Environments

One way to arouse our attention and reduce our perception of sameness is to give us more ways to personalize or put our own stamps on our travel living spaces. In this way, we can create more customized oases that speak to our own tastes and preferences.

Let's imagine that we were that business traveler who was staying in a room at a hotel that seemed acceptable but rather unremarkable and *hotel-like*. The challenge would be how to fashion accommodations in these types of settings to bring them more to life and make them appear more reflective of our own personality and style. A start might be to turn more power and control over to us to enable us to configure our room spaces in ways that we, not the hotel management, find particularly pleasing. For instance, we might be given more ability to precisely control our physical environment's basic comfort features such as the temperature settings in different parts of our room, the brightness and ambient glow of the various types of lights, or the black-out degree of our window drapes.

In addition to these kinds of simple comfort setting options, we could also be given opportunities to express our more aesthetic and personalized tastes. We might, for example, be offered some choices in such things as the color of the throw pillows we would like placed on our bed in the morning or the scent of the bath oil we would like left out on the bathroom counter. Some hotels offer guests modular furniture that can be rearranged in hotel room living spaces and, if we were in such a room, we might want to change the orientation of the desk or our reading chair to make it more comfortable for us. Maybe we could also select between complementary fuzzy or non-fuzzy slippers to wear, or choose between medium and light comforters or firm or soft pillows for sleeping. These kinds of choices, although rather small in themselves, could contribute to our sense that this was now, indeed, our own special place.

Choice, thus, empowers us and, particularly in western cultures, enables us to express our much valued individuality (Iyengar and Lepper 1999). In doing this, choice provides us with a sense that we and not others are in control, and that we have power over our environments. We also tend to like things more when we have had the chance to select them for ourselves as opposed to having someone else doing the choosing for us (Iyengar 2011). All of this adds to a *do-it-my-way* feeling of deep rightness in where we are and to an enhanced sense of autonomy and efficacy.

Personalization can be additionally fostered by travel providers using data gathered from our previous visits in order to anticipate what our likes and dislikes are apt to be on any of our repeat stays. This is often a feature of guest loyalty programs, which are designed to motivate us to return to the same places again and again (ReviewPro 2019). Thus, if we joined such a program and returned to the same hotel, or one in the same chain of hotels, a whole trove of data might be available from our first visit to help the hotel staff further customize services for us (Yeldell 2017). For instance, previous patterns of our service and amenity use, special requests, consumption habits, complaints, room service orders, dining practices, and so forth could be examined to predict our current needs and preferences. As just a few examples, if we utilized certain spa services on our last visit, we might be given some discount coupons for some similar spa packages during our current stay; if we previously requested a room with a view of the pool, we might be given a room with a similar pool view again; if we had some special dietary restrictions (e.g., we needed gluten-free food), items stocked in our room's complimentary snack baskets might be chosen to fit with these special needs; and if we liked cleaning services in the afternoon and/or late checkouts, arrangements could be made to accommodate these schedules, and so on.

The point is that very individualized guest experiences could be created by using either sophisticated data analysis methods or by simply giving us more freedom to choose to arrange our environments in ways that are especially pleasing to us. In each case, the hotel management would be honoring our unique requirements in order to provide us with experiences that are particularly comfortable and satisfying.

Questions for Discussion

Please work with the following questions in order to think more about factors that can produce non-responsiveness to surroundings when traveling. Also, consider the idea of the importance of personalization of travel spaces. For these questions, draw on your personal experiences as a traveler and/or on any experiences you have had in the travel industry.

1. Give an example of an experience that you enjoyed a lot at the beginning of one of your vacations (such as lying on a beach and doing nothing all day) that dulled as you repeated it over and over. Explain

this in terms of the concept of habituation. What, if anything, did you do to bring back some of your original delight in the experience?

2. What sorts of choices would you like to have available to you to be able to personalize your travel environments in ways that particularly suit you? Give some specific examples. Have you ever been in a travel situation where you had these kinds of choices and options? Did any of the personalizing suggestions offered in this chapter particularly resonate with you? Explain.

3. As we have seen, our travel environments can be increasingly customized for us on any repeat visits we might make to the same establishments through the use of data analytic procedures that track our habits and preferences from our first visits. Would having these customized amenities and service options in place for you give you an incentive to return to a particular place again? Why or why not? Can you see any downside to travel providers keeping records of your behavior and requests from previous visits? Explain.

4. What one idea stood out to you most in the material presented in this chapter? Discuss.

Notes

_____

_____

_____

_____

_____

_____

CHAPTER 11

Reducing Travel Habituation II

(or I Never Expected That Birthday Card!)

Kindness is the key that opens the door of favour and beautiful surprises.

—Michael Bassey Johnson

Chapter Preview

In this chapter, we continue to explore how to overcome our tendency for non-responsiveness to our travel environments. Here we look at how the travel provider can utilize surprises, kindness, and noticing in order to ameliorate patterns of habituation. Practical suggestions are also offered for how each of these strategies can best be implemented to enhance positive effects.

The Power of Surprises

The introduction of surprises into our environments is another way to jolt us out of our ho-hum reactions to our travel surroundings. Surprises can be effective because they are, by definition, unanticipated, unpredictable, and novel. They can pull our attention to them when we might otherwise be less responsive to our situations (Bryant and Veroff 2007).

To think about this, imagine how we would feel if small just-for-you gifts were occasionally left unexpectedly on our hotel or cruise ship room doors in the morning. These could be tailored to our particular personality tastes and interests. Or what if when we came back to our rooms after dinner each night, we would find different types and colors of candy put on our pillows, or if one day we received a notice that we won a surprise drawing for a free meal at a hotel restaurant or a free round of golf?

The key here would not be so much what is done, but the spirit with which it was done and the unexpectedness of the act. Every one of us, from elderly millionaires to young children, loves surprises and loves to receive unanticipated presents (Luna 2015). Indeed, we seem to especially value something given to us as an unforeseen gift if there appears to have been a great deal of thought behind the gift. This is, in part, because such gifts signal a warm intention and attitude toward us (Rigoglioso 2008). Thus, I will be apt to particularly cherish a gift such as a book of Emily Dickinson's poems that you bought me as a surprise present if I knew that you remembered that Emily Dickinson was my favorite poet. This is true both if the poetry book you gave me was one that was very expensively made or one that was not so expensive. Caring acts convey a sense of concern and interest in another person. With the addition of these types of small, caring gestures, a routine stay in what might have been a rather average and non-descript hotel could become for us a truly memorable experience.

Acts of Kindness

A caring attitude can also be expressed through general unsolicited acts of kindness (Filep, Macnaughton and Glover 2017). Being a recipient of kindness colors the way we see others and makes us feel that we are not so alone. A world filled with kindness becomes a gentler, more connected, and less cold place (Baskerville, Johnson, Monk-Turner, Slone, Standley, Stansbury, Williams and Young 2000). Kindness additionally begets kindness so that when we are the target of kind acts from others we tend, in turn, to be kinder to those with whom we interact, and we remember kind acts (Otake, Shimai, Tanaka-Matsumi, Otsui and Fredrickson 2006).

In this last regard, I think of a story that a friend told me about her visit to a beautiful hotel. On this particular occasion, my friend was celebrating her wedding anniversary, and her husband had a gorgeous bouquet of a dozen red roses delivered to their room. After some days, some of the flowers began to fade, and only one was left that still looked beautiful and fresh. My friend said she was reluctant to throw the flowers out because they reminded her of her husband's thoughtfulness to her, so she decided to keep the bouquet for one more day. After she and her husband came back from an afternoon of touring that day, she found that a housekeeper had placed the single stem rose that was still fresh in a new vase with a lovely ribbon tied around it. This bloom was placed on her dresser so that she could immediately see it when they entered the room. My friend said she almost cried when she noticed it, and she has never forgotten this incident or the name of the hotel where it took place.

Kindness stands out to people (Galante, Galante, Bekkers and Gallacher 2014). It touches them and gives them stories to tell long after they forget the color of the walls or the arrangement of furniture in the hotel lobby. And kindness often costs very little. It is the sort of gift that reciprocates for both the giver and receiver, and that lingers in an individual's mind long after the particular kindness event is over.

Noticing and Feeling Validated

A final gesture that can nudge us out of our non-responsiveness to our surroundings is the simple act of being noticed by another. Noticing expresses an attitude to the receiver that they are worthy of being listened to and of being seen (Seltzer 2017). This sort of *noticing* is what turns potentially forgettable experiences for us into ones that continue to resonate with us, and it can serve as a potent form of self-validation.

For instance, imagine a situation in which we have just checked into some type of lodging accommodations and, as we are leaving to go out again, the person at the check-in desk notices that it is raining and that we have no umbrella. Think of our reaction if this person at the desk jumped up and asked if we would like to borrow one of the hotel umbrellas as we leave the premises. Or, perhaps, a flight attendant on a long trip we are making overseas notices that our child is fidgeting in her seat and offers her a small toy to play with to ease our situation. In both of these instances, the other's reactions to us goes beyond simple scripted professionalism and, instead, becomes a case in which our particular situation and unique needs are taken into account.

As another example of this sort of noticing, I recall an incident that occurred during a stay my husband and I had many years ago in a lovely small hotel in Kolkata, India. My husband and I would go out every day to shop or see the famous sites and would return home at the end of the day rather tired. We got in the habit of buying and bringing to the room cold beers every afternoon after we returned from our touring. One day when we came back, we found two bottles of iced beer with an opener and two glasses provided by the hotel sitting on the table by our chairs. We, of course, were delighted, and we never forgot that experience. Long after some of the famous sites that we saw faded in our memories, that event stands out and remains strong in our minds. This small act of noticing turned what could have been simply a place to stay into a destination that felt like home and was forever fondly recalled.

Thus, noticing matters! It eases a feeling that is increasingly common in modern life that we are not really being seen in our interactions with others and have become faceless. A simple act of noticing can shift these types of perceptions, and this can be profoundly restorative to our sense of self. It affirms that others do, indeed, see us as being worthy of attention (Ariely, Kamenica and Prelac 2008). Noticing, it should be mentioned, is not the same as simply being polite or nice in a generic way. Rather, noticing occurs when someone responds to us as unique individuals with our own special needs, desires, and concerns. Such an act can be powerfully revitalizing.

Questions for Discussion

Please work with the following questions to think more about how surprises, acts of kindness, and noticing can pull us out of our non-responsiveness and non-receptivity to our travel surroundings. As you do this, draw on your personal experiences as a traveler and/or on any experiences you have had in the travel industry.

1. How would you define the concept of kindness? How is it different from simple politeness and friendliness? Do you think that people

in the hospitality industry (e.g., hotel staff, tour guides, etc.) could be trained to exhibit real kindness that goes beyond surface niceness? Why or why not? Would it be a good idea to try to do this?

2. Kindness often has an element of unscriptedness to it. It is a gift that we can give each other. In your experience, are most hotels/motels and/or other types of travel accommodations what you would call kind places in a deep sense? Have you had situations on some trips where staff exceeded superficial portrayals of kindness? Explain.

3. Surprises grab our attention. Think of a stay that you have had at a hotel when some type of unexpected or thoughtful surprise on the part of the hotel staff made your visit particularly memorable. Please describe what occurred. How might these kinds of surprises be integrated by travel providers more often into our typical travel experiences?

4. Being noticed and validated by others is particularly important in times such as ours when more and more people may be experiencing a sense of being lost in the crowd. Do you think in typical hotel stays we are made to feel noticed and validated? Why or why not? What would it take to make you feel this way?

Notes

_____

_____

_____

_____

_____

_____

CHAPTER 12

Facilitating Use of Time

(or Does the Pacing Seem a Bit Off Here?)

Time is an illusion, timing is an art.

—Stefan Emunds

Chapter Preview

In this chapter, the effective use of time to facilitate our trip enjoyment is discussed. Time is examined from several different perspectives. First, the significance of good pacing is discussed in terms of optimal arousal theory and the power of anticipation. Situations that allow time to be especially relished and the creation of bittersweet moments are also explored. Finally, the influence of proper time sequencing and the effects of saving the best until last are investigated.

The Power of Pacing

We have discussed how travel providers' reacting to us in a variety of affirmative ways can help pull us out of our non-responsiveness to our surroundings. Now we are going to shift topics and talk about how the travel provider's use of time can additionally affect how we perceive and take in our world. In particular, we will discuss how our responsiveness to our circumstances can be heightened by the perfect use of pacing in which services or other amenities are offered to us just when we are apt to be maximally receptive to them. We will call this the *just-right-moment* effect.

To think about this, imagine scenarios in which we and our friends visited two different restaurants on our vacation together. Imagine further that we all liked the dishes that we ordered so much in the first restaurant (Restaurant A) that we ordered the exact same dishes in the second restaurant (Restaurant B). Unfortunately, our reactions to the dishes, which were of equal quality, were quite different at the two restaurants. Let's take a look at what could have happened to produce such a difference.

In Restaurant A we all sat down at our favorite table and ordered appetizers, main courses, and then coffee and dessert to end our meal. After we talked for a while, just at the point when we were beginning to think about the appetizers we had ordered and how delicious they would taste, the waiter appeared with them and put them in front of us. The appetizers were, indeed, fantastic, and we relished each bite. When we finished our appetizers, we put our forks down and talked in a leisurely way for a while. Then, after a perfect amount of time, just before we were beginning to feel our first small pangs of hunger, our main courses arrived, and we ate our meals slowly, savoring each bite as we did. Following an appropriate interval, our dessert and coffee were then brought to us, which wonderfully capped off our dinners. We all left the restaurant feeling very satisfied and sated in a good way.

Now in contrast to the above, imagine Restaurant B where we all again were seated at our favorite table and ordered those same meals. Our appetizers this time came very quickly, and we were still trying to finish them when our main courses arrived. After a brief period of time, the waiter then came back and unceremoniously whisked away both of our first and main courses before we had finished either. Following all of this, we then had to wait 40 minutes to receive our dessert and coffee, which was long after we had any interest in either! When we finally left the restaurant, we felt miserable and angry, muttering that we would never patronize that particular establishment again!

We can easily surmise what happened to produce our different reactions to our restaurant experiences. Clearly, our positive or negative responses were related to how well or not well our meals were paced. Pacing can sometimes be either too slow or too fast, and its appropriateness has to do with our readiness to receive what is offered to us at the moment it is offered. Often getting this timing right in a dining context means servers have to allow sufficient (but not too long) pauses between food courses to enhance our enjoyment of our experience rather than making everything available too quickly or too slowly. Correct pacing relates to the power of anticipation to provoke excitement in what is to come. In this way, the joyfully anticipated experience is relished more than the always available one (Quoidbach, Mikolajczak and Gross 2015).

We can also think of good pacing in terms of the point at which we reach an optimal level of arousal where we are neither overwhelmed nor underwhelmed by our circumstances (Xie 2016). This was the moment in our first dining experience example in which the waiter appeared with the food just when we were hungry (but not too hungry). Here, each of us had just enough food served to us at just the right time.

Thus, pacing, when it is working, matches the customers' desires. This means that correct pacing does not always have to follow the same pattern for people in different types of circumstances (Noone, et al. 2007). For instance, a couple who has reservations to a theater performance right after their meal wants the spaces between their meal courses to be shorter than a couple who plans to make the experience of dining at a particular restaurant the only event in their evening out, or couples who are dining in high-end restaurants might well be more concerned with correct pacing than those eating in more casual fast-food type establishments (Noone, et al. 2007).

Furthermore, pacing is important not only in the serving of food but also in a myriad of other activities such as tour schedules, room cleaning services, entertainment venues, and the like. To give some examples, on guided tours we sometimes are hustled too quickly from site to site before we have a chance to really appreciate or assimilate what we are seeing, or we are stuck so long at one particular place that we grow bored listening to our tour guide talk about every detail of a particular site. A housekeeper may want to clean our rooms either so early in the morning that we are not yet awake when she arrives or so late in the afternoon that we thought she had forgotten about us entirely. This list could go on and on! Pacing is important because it is a crucial factor that leads either to relishing and being satisfied with our travel experiences or viewing them as encounters to be endured. It is an art to be learned by hospitality workers that has enormous consequences.

Time Sequencing and Saving the Best Until Last

How travel providers sequence events in other ways can also impact our travel satisfaction. We are often more conscious of the passage of time on vacations than we normally are because our vacation days are limited, and we never want them to end. This awareness of the fleetingness of time might seem like a depressing thought. Research, however, shows that our attention to time's passing can, ironically, heighten our pleasure in what we are doing by endowing events with what has been called a sense of the bittersweet (Lakein 1974). This sense is the feeling of sweet-sorrow that is intensified when we assume that events that we are particularly enjoying may never occur again (Larsen, McGraw and Cacioppo 2001). Understanding that this is the last time adds poignancy to our experiences and deepens their significance in our minds and memories.

To consider this, imagine that we were on a cruise on the last night of a journey. Perhaps, as happens on many tours, instead of downplaying the reality that the cruise will soon be over, our tour guide decides to commemorate this fact by holding a big *last night* special meal in the dining room for all the cruise passengers. By doing this, she wants to turn something that could have been potentially depressing into something that is particularly memorable.

Research shows that events occurring at the end of encounters hold a disproportionately powerful place in our minds when we reflect back on our experiences. According to the *peak and end rule*, we tend to most frequently remember what was best (or worst) about our experiences and what happened last (Do, Rupert and Wolford 2008). This means that if the party on the final day of our cruise was great, we are more apt to define our entire trip as being wonderful than if we had a great party in the middle of our adventure, but a depressing and tense last night. The lesson here for travel providers is that if they want to enhance positive memories of trips, they would be wise to try to end on a high note. Singers and entertainers have long known this. That is, if possible, they always attempt to save the best song or the best joke for last. It can also be helpful to make final events sufficiently different compared to what came before so that they can stand out in even more ways. For example, a comedian might end his comedy set with jokes that are very different in structure from his previous jokes. Or the cruise director who is arranging our last night meal might change some physical aspects of the dining room where the party is being held in order to make it look new and special. She might, for instance, place different types of flower arrangements on the tables where we sit, and/or change the color of the placemats and napkins or the arrangement of the tables and seats. She might have the band play different types of background music as we eat, or make the lighting in the room softer and more mysterious in feel than the previous lighting. In all these ways, something unique and particularly memorable could be created, images of which would long remain among our special travel memories.

Questions for Discussion

Please work with the following questions in order to think more about how to facilitate the use of time to enhance travel satisfaction. As you do this, draw on your own personal experience as a traveler and any experiences you may have had in the travel industry.

1. Good pacing, as we have seen, is very important to the creation of positive travel experiences. Think of some travel experiences (e.g., eating out, taking tours, etc.) that you have had that were either very well or not very well paced. Describe the difference. How did you feel after each experience?

2. How do you think people (e.g., waitresses, bartenders, housekeeping staff, front desk personnel, etc.) could best learn the art of good pacing and timing? What characteristics in staff might impede or facilitate their use of good pacing?

3. Endings are important because they frame and cap our experiences. What do you think a perfect ending to a stay at some type of vacation lodging would be like for you? What could the staff do to make your endings particularly special (beyond handling practical services well such as efficiently processing your bill, helping you with your luggage, getting you a cab, etc.)? Explain.

4. Endings can also be both happy and sad at the same time. In other words, they can be bittersweet. Have you ever experienced these

kinds of bittersweet moments during your travels? If yes, explain. Brainstorm how people in the hospitality industry could help create more of these kinds of moments.

5. What one common mistake do you think people in the hospitality industry often make regarding pacing? Explain.

Notes

_____

_____

_____

_____

_____

_____

CHAPTER 13

Promoting Traveler Engagement

(or I am So Into This!)

Release your creative energy and let it flow. Relish the possibilities.
—Nita Leland

Chapter Preview

In this chapter, the framework of psychological flow is utilized to discuss how to promote our full engagement in trip activities and experiences. Flow occurs when we are so completely immersed in what we are doing that we can devote all our effort and attention to our task with no superfluous expenditures of energy. Conditions are then explored that facilitate or impede the creation of flow, as well as strategies travel providers could use to help us achieve flow states.

Engagement and Well-Being

We have talked about different ways in which we might be nudged into states of greater awareness and receptiveness to our surroundings, and we have looked at some of the challenges involved in doing this. The goal is to enable us to be completely present in our environment and fully engaged in our encounters in it. Such engagement has been defined as an important component of well-being, and to experience it can be extremely satisfying. Research, in fact, has shown the power of the right activities to absorb and energize us and facilitate a myriad of positive emotions (Massimini and Carli 1988). These emotions do not consist of short-term or fleeting sensations of pleasure that can come and go quickly, but rather of the deeper and more lasting feelings of contentment and fulfillment that come with doing things we love to do with complete commitment and attention. Let's consider some more how such states and the positive emotions that accompany them might be achieved in traveling.

Travel and Flow

Travel, as we have seen, gives us opportunities to try new things and interact with the world in ways that are especially meaningful to us. Through this process, a new sense of vigor in our lives can be restored. To consider this more, imagine that we were on vacation paddling a kayak in a beautiful lagoon or taking pictures of a sunset. Imagine, further, that we became so engaged with what we were doing that time for us seemed to disappear and simply fly by. In fact, maybe we became so intrigued by our tasks that we lost consciousness of ourselves and just concentrated on what we were attempting to do, not how we looked doing it. Although working on our tasks took all of our effort and focus, when we were finished, in addition to feeling a bit fatigued, we also felt very energized, alive, and filled with a sense of well-being.

The preceding description portrays a state of being that psychologists have described as a *flow state* (Massimini and Carli 1988; Csikszentmihalyi 1990). This state occurs when we are so totally in the moment and in sync with what we are doing that we can fully devote all our energy to the task at hand (Jackson 1992). To obtain a mental picture of this, imagine a dancer who is completely immersed in his performance at some moment, a painter who is completely absorbed in the picture she is creating, or a ball player who is not just playing ball but who has become one with the game he is in and seems to exhibit a sense of effortlessness in his play. Similar to a cat in a chase, in these states energy seems to beget energy with no superfluous expenditures, and we become totally consumed by the actions we are taking.

Experiencing flow, thus, consists of a very positive feeling of being completely drawn into and taken up by by what we are doing. The question of relevance here is how we can find these types of flow moments more often when we travel and how travel providers can help us in this task.

Conditions for Flow

While flow can't be willed into being, conditions can be set up that are likely to either promote or interfere with it occurring (Csikszentmihalyi 1990). For one thing, we know that flow more often occurs when we are doing something active that requires effort rather than participating in more passive activities. Thus, when we are simply sitting in our hotel rooms watching TV or looking out the window daydreaming, we would not be likely to be experiencing flow. Flow involves a more focused kind of trying.

To find flow, we also have to have tasks made available to us that particularly engage us and are at the right level of challenge for our skill level (Moneta and Csikszentmihalyi 1996). Thus, if we are a middle-level tennis player who was looking for a memorable tennis game, we would probably not want to try to play with either a star player or with a person who just started learning tennis who has trouble hitting back simple serves. The first person would be likely to overwhelm us, while the second would probably bore us.

We also would be benefitted if we could find an environment in which we can feel relaxed and at ease and not too self-conscious (Grenville-Cleave 2013). This is particularly true if we are the kind of person who tends to be very self-aware in public. In such a case, having a critical audience watch us as we attempt to learn some difficult new skills would most likely not contribute to our ability to concentrate on what we were doing. Needless to say, negative comparisons are the guaranteed killers of flow.

Finally, flow seems to be more easily achieved when we have clear goals and clear feedback about our performance (Strati, Shernoff and Kackar 2012). If, for example, we were trying to put together floral bouquets in a flower arranging class with no clear objectives and no clear feedback about how well we were doing, we would be apt to soon lose interest in our project. On the other hand, if we had a teacher or a guide who set in place objectives for us, and who gave us clear feedback on how well we were meeting those objectives as well as concrete ideas on what we might do to improve our skills, our chances for staying engaged in our task would increase. Such feedback would be best if it was neither so negative that it demoralized us nor so generally positive that it gave us no specific directions about how to make our flower arrangements better. Thus, after we completed our assignment instead of the teacher saying to us something generally disheartening such as "I don't think your arrangement works" or something generically supportive such as "That looks great," it would be better if she gave clear ideas about where and how we might change our work to improve it. For instance, she might say something like, "I think if you added some color by putting in a sprig of these deep crimson berries and then created variations in the height of your flowers, the whole arrangement would be more balanced."

Helping Travelers Find Flow

Thus, although there are no simple formulas for finding specific kinds of activities and environments that are guaranteed to promote flow, there are certain conditions that can facilitate or hinder the probability of a flow state occurring. Of course, perfect environments that might facilitate achieving a flow state for one person may be different for another person depending on personality profiles and individual strengths and preferences. This again comes down to the idea of fit. For instance, on a personal note, I enjoy both oil painting and playing the mandolin. If I planned to continue to pursue these activities on some vacation, I would much prefer to work one-on-one with a teacher rather than joining a large group or class. I would also hope to have a teacher who had worked with people of many different skill levels, not just with professional artists or musicians. Finally, it would be helpful if the teacher liked to paint still life pictures and was known for being able to give comments to his or her students in a useful but also non-evaluative manner.

The above preferences could be considered my flow profile: other people may well have different preferences. Note that such preferences do not relate to some abstract interests we have such as an in interest in politics or in movies. They are also not statements of things we somewhat like to do or think we should like to do. Rather our flow profiles specify what kinds of tasks completely absorb us while working on them, and what kinds of circumstances tend to be present when this happens. Once we had identified these tasks and our situational requirements for pursuing them, travel staff such as trip planners, hotel concierges, or cruise directors could assist us in finding appropriate places or venues near our destination sites where they might optimally be carried out.

Coming back to my personal case, after I expressed my interest in art and discussed what I was looking for in an art teacher with my travel provider, he or she could tell me about artists in the nearby community who often work at home or who teach still life oil painting to students who are both beginners and more advanced. Perhaps, he or she could additionally share with me any reviews that were available about these artists and inform me about the techniques or methods they use to instruct their students. I might even be provided with some photos of the different artists' work, if they were available. Reviewing this kind of information would allow me to make more informed choices about the types of teaching venues that would be most likely to work for me, which would considerably add to my ability to find enjoyment and pleasure on my trip.

Questions for Discussion

Please work with the following questions to think more about how we can find activities and experiences on our trips that are engaging and energizing. Draw on your own personal experiences as a traveler and/or any experiences you may have had in the travel industry as you do this.

1. Being energized by a task or finding flow has been described as a sort of effortless effort. What does this mean to you? Have you ever personally experienced such a state? Describe.
2. Do you think typical amenities and services offered in hotels and other types of lodgings (e.g., gyms, pool areas, reading rooms, recreational areas, etc.) are apt to be conducive to the creation of flow? Using some of the ideas presented in this chapter and your own experiences, consider how travel environments could better facilitate flow.
3. How might a hotel concierge or other hotel personnel best work with us to identify activities that would engage us? What would your own flow profile look like?

4. What, in your opinion, is the most common obstacle to finding flow that you and other travelers often face in travel situations? Consider things like physical distractions and noise, crowded conditions, others' evaluative attitudes, inappropriate challenge levels, and so on.

Notes

_____

_____

_____

_____

_____

_____

CHAPTER 14

Enhancing Experiences of Awe

(or Wow, I Am Breathless!)

Most of the time beauty lies in the simplest of things.
—Winna Efendi

Chapter Preview

In this chapter, the nature of awe as an experience that sometimes occurs in travel is discussed. Factors that facilitate or impede finding awe are also explored, as well as strategies that travel professionals can use to promote its occurrence.

The Nature of Awe

Traveling, as we have seen, can cause us to experience many different emotions that we do not encounter as much in our day-to-day routines, including the experience of awe. Awe occurs when we ponder something that seems magnificent and wondrous to us, and that in some ways defies our normal categories of description (Allen 2018). It leaves us feeling speechless and can temporality take us out of ourselves (Maslow 1968). It is, in fact, this very self-diminishing aspect of awe that is part of its power. We feel small in a good way because something else seems so grand, large, or exceptionally excellent (Keltner and Haidt 2003).

For example, we may experience a kind of awe as we gaze at something like the Grand Canyon or look at the vastness of an ocean. We may stare at the deep, magnificent blue of some of the colors of stained glass windows in ancient cathedrals or listen to the sounds of a wonderful symphony and really hear it in its full beauty for the first time. When these moments occur, a sort of *ah* feeling is created that remains stamped in our memories. These experiences can literally take our breath away and give us chills or goose bumps. They can also be transformative in the sense that witnessing something with awe can leave us feeling that we now understand some aspect of our world in a new and expanded way (Elkins 2001). Long after we have forgotten what restaurants we may have eaten in or what train we took to such and such a place, these kinds of experiences of awe stay vivid and bright in our minds.

Experiencing awe is also connected to many positive emotions. For instance, awe facilities a feeling of connection to others and a sense that we are somehow all privileged to be in this magnificent world together (Krause and Hayward 2014). Similar to the flow states that we talked about in the Chapter 13, awe also leads to a kind of self-emptying in which we are temporality unconcerned with ourselves and less burdened by our own issues and problems (Shiota, Keltner and Steiner 2007). In this way, experiencing awe can be very psychologically therapeutic. Awe additionally increases our tendencies to be kind and generous to others, because awe is associated with a feeling of social embeddedness and relatedness.

Although feeling awe is a deeply satisfying experience, sometimes this state is difficult to achieve. To go back to our Grand Canyon example, a trip there could end up being either a magnificent highlight of our lives or a miserable time to endure, depending on many of the factors we have already discussed in this book. For instance, simple exhaustion can interfere with our ability to feel awe and be responsive and receptive to our surroundings. Thus, if we saw the Grand Canyon after a long and tiring trip followed by insufficient sleep, it would be unlikely that we would be able to completely appreciate its beauty. This sort of travel fatigue can be compounded by trying to adhere to schedules that are overcrowded and inappropriately paced, as would likely be the case if we tried to view the entire Grand Canyon, which is huge, as one stop in a multi-stop day of traveling. Our receptivity to awe can be further diminished by engaging in negative comparisons with others that take away our focus on what we, ourselves, are doing or experiencing. As an example of this, imagine that we arrive at the Grand Canyon only to notice that everyone but us seemed to have secured private tour guides to lead them to the most famous parts of the Canyon, or had tickets on a bus to take them to key viewing sites. If we spent our entire day obsessing about this, we might fail to take in the glory of what was right before our eyes. Finally, our ability to experience awe can also be undermined by our cultivation of a ho-hum attitude toward the world that we described earlier, where we feel like we have seen it all and are convinced that nothing is left that can impress us.

Awe, then, while a glorious feeling, can be easily snuffed out if our trips are not structured correctly. This is, again, where good travel planners and providers can be useful. As we have seen, travel professionals can help us organize trips that are not overly tiring and that are well paced. They can assist us in securing accommodations that are restful, and that even include options for restorative spa experiences. Travel planners and providers can also give us access to useful practical information about such things as how we can secure or book tour guides, if we want them, or how we can obtain site transportation tickets, if we need them. Doing these sorts of things in advance would diminish feelings of confusion and uncertainty, which could take away from our ability to fully appreciate the beauty and grandeur that we encounter on our trips, something none of us wants to occur.

Questions for Discussion

Please answer the following questions to think more about the power of awe to add to experiences of travel joy. For these questions, draw on your personal experiences as a traveler and/or on any experiences you have had in the travel industry.

1. Have you ever experienced awe as it was defined in this chapter on some trip that you took in the past? If yes, describe the experience.
2. What do you think prevents us from experiencing awe more during our travels? Explain. What has prevented you from experiencing awe on a past trip?
3. Which of the suggestions for things travel providers might do to promote our ability to experience awe were most interesting to you?

Explain. Are there any other strategies that travel providers might use to promote awe that were not brought up in this chapter? If yes, please describe.

4. Do you think, in general, we are a culture that values regarding our surroundings with awe? Why or why not?

Notes

_____

_____

_____

_____

_____

Case Study 2:
The Actual Trip

You have just read many ideas about how satisfactory experiences during travel can best be facilitated and about the types of obstacles that can prevent this from occurring. Now you will have a chance to apply some of the ideas presented in Part II of the book to a hypothetical case study. Doing this will allow you to more actively work with the concepts to which you have been exposed and to integrate them more effectively to solve real-life types of travel dilemmas. There are no right or wrong answers here, so do not be held back by searching for the so-called correct solutions. Just try to draw on your own experiences and on the frameworks that were provided to critically analyze the presented case.

The Story of Peter

Imagine that you have a friend named Peter who has traveled widely around the world for business purposes. Recently, Peter and his wife took a trip for pleasure to the city of San Francisco. They stayed at a top-rated hotel in the heart of the city where all of the rooms had a beautiful view of the San Francisco skyline. The hotel had a lovely lobby and a gorgeous bar, as well as a highly regarded restaurant on the grounds. Despite all of this, Peter reported to you that his lodging experience was not particularly memorable to him, and that he and his wife just did not seem to fit in with the hotel. It was all too slick and cool for them. Everything was very predictable, and he said it looked just like a million other hotels they had been to in the past. Their room was decorated with impeccable taste, but felt impersonal to them. All the staff appeared to be extremely busy and had little time for interactions with guests. Peter said that nothing they did on their trip really engaged them because nothing appealed to their personal interests. They had simply visited a group of top sites in the city from a list that the hotel concierge had given them on their arrival.

Meals in the hotel restaurant were correctly served but had a little rushed *get-through* feeling about them. Peter, who had arrived at the hotel with his wife after a long and exhausting flight from the East Coast, said he and his wife felt tired when they arrived and fatigued rather than rejuvenated when they left to return to their home on the last day of their visit.

Imagine now that you were hired as a travel industry consultant to help the managers of this hotel make their guests' experiences with them feel more special. Using some of the ideas from the preceding chapters, and your own experiences as a traveler and/or travel professional, brainstorm about some things you might suggest to this hotel manager to make this couple's experience more memorable. What kinds of questions would you ask the hotel staff about how they typically do things? What sort of information would you like to know about this couple to help make their stay more pleasant? What types of changes might you tell hotel staff to consider? How might the staff alter what your friend referred to as the somewhat cold atmosphere of this hotel? Come up with all of the suggestions you can think of that would make this hotel stand out more from others and facilitate positive and memorable stays.

Notes

PART III

Post-Trip Well-being

Travel is a new experience that can transport you out of your everyday routine to create memories with the ones you love.

—Brian Chesky

In this part of the book, we will talk about how we can use the post-trip period to heighten and prolong the positive impact of our travels. Similar to anticipating our trips before they take place, remembering trips after they are over can enhance and intensify the pleasure we obtain from them. Even though our physical trips are long behind us, memories of them can linger in our minds, and these memories can be an important part of our delight in our total trip experience (Fridgen 1984). We remember because we want to hold onto and bring back something that was meaningful to us (Selstad 2007; Cary 2004; Pearce 2005). Reflecting on memories allows us to extend our joy in our experiences and can provide us with endless sources of well-being (Hammitt 1980).

Let's now consider more about what we can do to evoke nourishing trip memories and how travel providers might work with us in this effort. As we do this, we will talk about multiple ways of enhancing our post-trip reflections that speak to our different interests and styles. For instance, we will look at: the power of physical mementos, the joy of sharing stories, the insights gained from verbal reflection and journaling, and the pleasure of extending and deepening knowledge in new directions.

CHAPTER 15

Supporting Use of Mementos

(or Why Is This Little Seashell So Special to Me?)

Memory is the scribe of the soul.

—Aristotle

Chapter Preview

The use of mementos to prompt our positive post-trip reflections is discussed in this chapter. Mementos can take many forms, from saved pictures of beautiful places we visited to recordings of favorite musical performances we heard. Even seemingly small mementos can spark recollections of particularly memorable trip moments and, in this way, keep them fresh in our minds. Strategies that travel providers can use to work with us in this memento gathering process are also explored.

The Power of Mementos

Research has shown that we use all our senses to trigger remembrances (Rettner 2010). For example, listening again to music we heard on a trip, smelling the scents of flowers or spices we encountered during our journeys, or looking at pictures we took of beautiful places that we visited can all prompt a kind of positive reflection and a re-relishing of special trip occurrences (Stylianou-Lambert 2012). Physical mementos are important because we sometimes overestimate how vivid our experiences will remain in our minds. By reminiscing with mementos, we can keep fresh what otherwise might have been a quickly disappearing, forgotten moment (Mossberg 2007).

We may think that the best mementos to gather to spark trip remembrances would be the ones that are the fanciest or the most expensive. But research, in fact, suggests that rather than bringing back home big flashy souvenirs, it is often better to simply collect small items from our trips that have a particular story or some meaningful associations connected to them (Weiss 2016). For instance, we might collect some beautiful pinecones that we found on our vacation during a wonderful hike that we took in the woods, or we may take a seashell with us that we spotted on the beach on a romantic anniversary trip. Then, when we later examine the pinecone or look at the seashell, we can take ourselves back in time to relive these special moments again and again.

Helping to Spark Recollections: The Unique Gift

Of course, mementos can take an infinite variety of forms, and travel providers themselves might assist us in using them to bring back our travel reminisces. As we know, often it is the thought behind the mementos rather than the objective quality of the mementos themselves that makes them something to be cherished. For example, imagine that we had stayed at a certain small hotel somewhere that was enclosed by a beautiful rose garden. Perhaps, when we paid our bill at the end of our stay at this hotel, a single silk rose was included with our receipt. This type of thoughtful gesture, though quite insignificant in itself, could transform something like a routine bill-paying interaction into an encounter that suddenly stood out and became memorable. By looking at the rose later, positive reminiscences of our trip could be evoked, and particular memories associated with this hotel where we stayed could come to mind. Thus, a seemingly small gift could have a rather lasting impact and could lead to many return visits to this special place.

The power that these kinds of unexpected gift mementos can have on us makes me think of a particular personal story. In this case, my husband and I were staying in a small, somewhat non-descript motel that was located in the middle of a town that had a gift shop that specialized in selling little rubber ducks of the sort that children sometimes use at bath time. On the last day of our stay at this motel, we found one of these little play duckies left on the side of the tub in our bathroom with a note that said, "Take me, my dear friend, to remind you where you've been and hopefully where you will soon return." When we went out into the hall to thank the housekeeper who had left it there, she just smiled, and we noticed that in the cart that she was pushing around, in addition to her cleaning supplies and pillows and towels, she had a whole bin of these little ducks. This, of course, made us laugh, but we did take the small duck with us, and we still have it placed on the edge of our bathtub at home. Thus, from this one somewhat silly and whimsical gesture, a motel stay that would probably have been long forgotten by us was transformed into one that we remember fondly to this day. As a coda to this story, I should add that we have returned to stay again at that motel—and joyfully received another rubber duck! There was a comfort in getting back to the same lodging; we knew the plan of the place, where the ice machine was, where and how amenities could be accessed, and so forth. This comfort was doubly enhanced when special treats were again provided, which were unique and which, best of all, made us smile.

Creating Scenes

Besides giving us special and unusual gifts to take home, travel providers might also work collaboratively with us in other ways to help us create lasting memories. One thing many of us like to do these days is to memorialize our trip experiences by taking pictures or videos of scenes that have special resonance or meaning for us, and then posting these images on social media platforms like Instagram or Facebook for us and others to view. Travel providers could assist us in this task by making available backdrops and images for our pictures that are particularly notable (Digital Memories 2018). Restaurant chefs, for instance, knowing that many of us like to take and then post pictures of meals that we have had on special occasions, could make sure that their food presentations are instagramable or visually outstanding as well as tasty to eat. Hotel designers could help us find share-worthy scenes by creating physical spaces that are especially beautiful such as lobbies with artfully decorated walls or atriums with majestic waterfalls (Instagram Best Practices 2020).

Share-worthy scenes could additionally be created from moments that were psychologically rather than simply ascetically significant for us.

For instance, we might find it interesting to post pictures of unexpected surprises and/or kindnesses that we encountered during our trips such as the housekeeper having turned down our bed in preparation for our sleep each night, or a waiter having sung Happy Birthday to us after we dined at the hotel restaurant. These types of posts would chronicle moments that we felt were distinctive and personally satisfying and would represent special aspects of the hotel's service to us. Such posts would not only serve to prompt our own later event recollections, but also, with our permission, could be put up on the hotel's website to advertise how this hotel was different and unique in terms of the considerateness and the personal attentiveness with which they treated their guests (Hotels Finding Ways 2018).

The preceding are examples of what is called user-generated content (UGC). UGC concerns material produced by guests who patronize different types of travel establishments, as opposed to content put out by professional staff. Studies have shown (Morris 2019) that we tend to particularly trust this type of user-generated information because we believe that it gives us especially accurate depictions of what it would really be like to stay in a particular place or eat at a particular restaurant. Such content not only enhances our own memories of our trip's special moments, but additionally can be used as a powerful marketing tool for travel providers to advertise what is extraordinary about their particular offerings.

Questions for Discussion

Please work with the following questions to think more about the power of mementos to enhance post-trip reflections. Draw on your own personal travel experiences and/or any experiences you have had in the travel industry as you do this.

1. What types of mementos have you brought back from your own trips? Which ones were especially meaningful to you? Why?
2. Have you ever been given something by someone in the travel industry (e.g., a copy of a menu, a postcard, a pen, etc.) that you kept as a special memento of the place that you visited? What kinds of things

do you think it would be fun to receive from travel providers to remind you of your trips? Explain.

3. In this chapter, the special quality of small, personal mementos to evoke memories was discussed. These types of mementos can range from such things as a seashell collected from a beautiful beach that you visited to a recording of birdsong from a gorgeous forest in which you hiked. Using both your own experiences and the suggestions offered in the reading, how do you think travel providers might work collaboratively with us to help us collect these types of special mementos?

4. We can also spark remembrance by capturing trip images that can later be posted on social media. Again, using your own experience and the suggestions given in this chapter, how could travel providers work with us to create posts that were particularly memorable and unique?

5. Would you like opportunities to have some of your own posts featured on the websites of hotels where you stayed in order to give other travelers a chance to see what your travel experiences at these places were like? Why or why not?

Notes

_____

_____

_____

_____

_____

_____

CHAPTER 16

Helping Travel Story Sharing

(or Did That Happen to You Too?)

Traveling—it leaves you speechless, then turns you into a storyteller.
—Ibn Battuta

Chapter Preview

In this chapter the use of shared travel storytelling to enrich our reflections of our trip experiences is discussed. Such storytelling can provide us with new perspectives on the meaning of our experiences and can make our memories of them more vivid. Strategies that travel providers could use to work collaboratively with us to facilitate these kinds of memory-sharing conversations are then explored.

Stories to Tell: Forming Bonds With Others and Gaining Insights

Sharing stories of our travels, particularly with those who have participated with us on our travel adventures, can have many positive effects. As some authors have noted, our story of our trip actually consists of multiple stories (Skinner and Theodossopoulos 2011). The first story is the trip that we initially imagined, the second is the trip that we actually took, and the third is the trip that we later reconstructed (Sutton 1992). In this reconstruction process, talking to other co-travelers is most helpful because as we compare notes and ideas, we can sometimes identify themes of meaning and significance that might have less readily occurred to us on our own (Kumar and Gilovich 2015). Sharing stories with others can additionally add a certain freshness and color to our travel recollections (Walker, Skowronski and Thompson 2003). Others can help us fill in that which we forgot and enable us to build upon that which we recalled. Through this process, more comprehensive and more finely elaborated pictures of our experiences can emerge (Bryant, Chadwick and Kluwe 2011).

For instance, we may have forgotten, until we talked with a friend who made journeys similar to ours, what cakes and coffee tasted like during late afternoon *kaffe und kuchen* times in Germany, or what the colors of the rocks looked like in the setting sun in an Arizona desert. Hearing these kinds of events described by someone else allows us to see our experiences again through the eyes of another, and this can add a wonderful layer of fresh appreciation to our reminiscences.

Facilitating Storytelling

The process of telling travel stories, then, can help us reimagine in a new light what our travel adventures meant to us. One way to reminisce with stories is to simply draw on our own memories to bring our trip experiences back to mind. Another way is to reconnect once again after our travels are over with the other travelers with whom we shared our experiences. It is in this reconnection process that travel providers can be particularly helpful. To mention just a few options, travel providers could provide post-trip access to some sorts of online discussion forums to link us together with those who participated in similar travel activities such as eating meals at the same restaurant during a cruise or taking part in the same guided tours during some wilderness outings. In these forums, we could either be given the chance to engage in open and unprompted reminiscing or the travel providers could more actively spark our memories by describing specific events that had taken place during our times together (Digital Memories 2018).

We could additionally be provided with incentives to share our stories. For instance, *Tell Us Your Story* links could be placed on hotel websites where we could earn certain kinds of travel reward points for posting descriptions of the travel adventures we had while staying at a particular hotel. Games could also be created where we could win different types of amenities on any return visits by coming up with the most hotel-related travel memories. Beyond giving us opportunities to recall and reminisce about our trips, such sites could also serve as rich sources of information for travel providers themselves to learn what types of encounters were the most memorable and what kinds of situations and experiences were liked best and least.

When I think of this, I remember the time my husband and I spent on a year-long scholarship in South Asia. Before we departed for our various assignments, all the individuals who were to be on this scholarship year were given special orientation sessions about South Asia. Then, over the course of the year, we would all periodically meet to check in with the scholarship staff and each other. These reunion sessions were filled with wonderful laughter and "Can you believe?" and "Did this happen to you too?" moments. Sharing our stories not only made us feel closer to other individuals who were on the scholarship year with us, but also connected us more affectionately to the program staff. We became a band of like-minded adventurers who forged a common understanding and knowledge about certain things that became quite meaningful to us. This is the kind of bond that makes for lasting memories and deep attachments, and it would not take a year-long trip in Asia to facilitate such feelings.

Questions for Discussion

Please work with the following questions to think more about the use of storytelling to spark trip memories and to add new perspectives on a trip's meaning. As you do this, draw both on your own personal travel experiences and/or any experiences you may have had in the travel industry.

1. Telling stories can help us solidify our memories of our travels and can enable us to strengthen our bonds with the people with whom we shared experiences. Have you ever had this sense of bonding emerge after you swapped travel stories with others? Explain.
2. How might people in the hospitality industry facilitate this kind of shared travel storytelling among us? Which of the suggestions offered in this chapter to promote storytelling were most interesting to you? Explain.

3. What makes swapping stories with others who have undergone similar travel encounters so compelling and interesting to us?

4. Do you think we are apt to be more positively influenced by spontaneous stories told from fellow travelers about their experiences in different travel settings, as opposed to advertising campaigns about these settings from hospitality industry professionals? If yes, why would this be the case?

Notes

_____

_____

_____

_____

_____

_____

CHAPTER 17

Promoting Travel Journaling

(or I Never Want to Throw My Trip Diary Away!)

I never travel without my diary. One should always have something sensational to read in the train.

—Oscar Wilde

Chapter Preview

In this chapter, the use of journaling to facilitate reminisces about our trip experiences is discussed. Journaling can be carried out through a variety of methods ranging from making handwritten entries in a diary to constructing vlogs (video blogs) and/or other types of recorded travel documentaries. Journaling is particularly effective in sparking trip reflections because it allows us to create ongoing and evolving records of our trip impressions. It is a skill that can be facilitated by our travel providers as they work with us in different ways.

The Power of Journaling

Many of us like to keep some type of documentary records or journals on our trips of what we have seen and done so that the experiences we have had are not forgotten. Unlike single pictures which only capture individual moments in time, the act of journaling permits the construction of ongoing narrative reflections of our trip encounters. Journaling allows us to capture our reactions to things when our impressions are fresh and unfiltered, and reviewing such reactions when we return home enables us to see what we saw in our travels over again and to gain new insights about them (Levine 2018).

Journal entries are particularly interesting to use to evoke travel reminiscences because they give us a chance to relive our experiences as they occurred in real time. We may, for instance, be surprised when we re-read our journal or review our vlog (Doherty 2018) to learn that our first impression of seeing Times Square in New York City was that all the people looked a bit bizarre, or that what impressed us most about Niagara Falls on the day that we saw it was not the visual beauty of the falls, but rather the tremendous power of the sound of the water splashing over the rocks and hitting the bottom of the falls. Further, by reviewing journal records, we can also learn if and how our impressions have shifted and changed over the length of our journeys. Perhaps, for example, on the first day of our trip, we noted that we were quite overwhelmed by New York City, but on the last day, we wrote that we were much more relaxed about being there. Maybe we forgot until we looked at our journal again that we felt sad and lonely at the beginning of our cruise but happy and energized by the end, or that early on in our travels to some place, we thought that the people in the culture we were visiting seemed a bit lazy, but that we modified this view as we got to know them better. Journaling, then, can serve not only as a means of factually documenting what we did or what we saw, but also can act as an aid to help us understand how our impressions evolved through time as we continually reacted and responded to new experiences (Carpenter 2001).

The act of keeping journals during trips also offers advantages to us in other ways. Journaling allows us to step back and see the larger picture that we may have missed in some of the hustle and bustle associated with the practicalities of our travels (Barth 2018). It can promote a kind of perspective-taking and thoughtfulness about experiences that can deepen our pleasure in them. In fact, the very act of keeping journals can facilitate a kind of heightened attentiveness to our surroundings (Amabile and Kramer 2011). This is because the knowledge that we will later write down or verbally record our trip impressions causes us to look more attentively at our environments in the moment as we attempt to discern patterns and meaning in what we see. Journaling additionally helps us decide what we would like to further experience or not experience on our present or future trips.

Facilitating Journaling

The act of writing about or in other ways creating narrative versions of our travel experiences, thus, has many benefits. This powerful tool is something that we would be wise to cultivate, and is a skill that could be facilitated by those in the travel industry. Although it is not hard for us to simply record impressions of our trips these days because of all of the devices we have at our disposal, ranging from simple notebooks to cell phones and iPads, it can be more difficult for us to know how to make our records memorable, interesting, and creative. Here is where travel providers could be helpful.

First, travel providers could make available to us rich background information to heighten our understanding of what we are observing during our journeys. As just a few examples, a guide at some geological site could help us better appreciate the majesty and magnificence of what we were seeing by noting that the rock formations in front of us had taken over a billion years to form and contained multiple fossils from animals long since extinct on earth. Or before attending events like concerts or special dinners, we could be given opportunities to meet backstage with the musicians who will be performing in the concerts or with the chefs who will be preparing our meals. All of this could then enrich our later reflections on the meaning of our experiences.

We could additionally be taught, in general, how to simply become more sensitive observers of our environments. For instance, if we were getting ready to take a hike in a beautiful forest, we could be shown how to recognize the calls of various types of birds present in that forest, or how to pick out the scent of different types of flowers. Those of us preparing to stroll along a beach could be shown how to recognize small shells that are often found in the sand there, or how to identify tide patterns in the sea. Such training would heighten our ability to be mindfully receptive to our surroundings and to be able to later create narratives about our experiences that were nuanced and perceptive. These are the kinds of narratives that tend to stay with us and to make us long to return again and again to the place where they were created.

Questions for Discussion

Please answer the following questions to think more about how journaling can help you coalesce and bring to life meaningful travel experiences that you have had. Draw on both your personal travel experiences and/or any experiences you have had in the travel industry as you do this.

1. Have you ever kept a written journal or made an audio or video record of some trip that you took? If yes, did doing so impact how you remembered your trip later? Explain.
2. How do you think the sorts of memories evoked by reviewing trip journals (either written, audio, or video) tend to be different from those evoked by looking at individual photos of trip moments? Explain.
3. Vlogs and other types of travel journaling are becoming increasingly popular today. Which of the suggestions offered in this chapter about how people in the travel industry could work with us to help us create more nuanced and perceptive records of our trips were the most interesting to you? Why? Are there other types of assistance you would like to receive from travel providers if you decided to try to keep some sort of journals on your next travel outing? Describe.
4. What makes for a good journal entry in your opinions? What elements does it have? How is good journaling different from simple description?

Notes

_____

_____

_____

_____

_____

CHAPTER 18

Assisting in Post-Trip Knowledge Extension

(or I Am Just Learning More and More About This!)

Still around the corner there may wait, a new road or a secret gate.
—J.R.R. Tolkien

Chapter Preview

In this chapter opportunities that travel provides for us to continue to explore and extend our knowledge in new directions after we return home from our trips are discussed. The ways that travel providers could work with us in these pursuits of further knowledge are also examined. The key idea is that the rewards of travel do not have to end when our trips are over, but rather can endure long into the future.

Continuing to Learn and Explore

Traveling gives us opportunities to learn about the world in new ways, and when we return from our trips, we can continue to build on that learning. (Davidson-Hunt and Berkes 2003; Pearce and Foster 2007). Extending our knowledge in this way can increase the joy obtained from traveling and can lead us in new and fun explorative directions. As an example of this, consider the following scenario.

Let's imagine that we had an opportunity to visit some beautiful caves on a trip we took to the American West, and that this experience made us decide to take up the study of caves as a new hobby after we returned home. To begin to pursue our hobby, we decided to read more about caves and, through this process, we learned to appreciate the wonders of different types of rock formations found in them. We also visited several natural history museums that featured exhibitions on caves and learned about types of animal life and fossil remains that can be discovered in their dark recesses. In our studies, we further came across some amazing examples of beautiful cave paintings by early humans and became quite intrigued by this. Acquiring all this knowledge then gave us a new, more sophisticated framework for thinking about caves, in general, and motivated us to want return to the site of our original cave explorations again and again so that we could view what we first witnessed there with more discerning eyes and visit other caves in the vicinity. Thus, what began as one small experience on one particular trip blossomed into a passionate hobby that continued to take us in all sorts of interesting new directions.

Although the above story is hypothetical, the point is that the impact of travel can go on and on as we seek out new learning related to our different trip experiences. Travel providers could help us in this process by providing us with resources to use to guide our continued post-trip explorations. For instance, travel providers could make available to us links to bibliographies of readings or to lists of movies or documentaries on different topics related to sites that we visited on our trips. Depending on our preferences, we could also be informed about how to contact local people at our travel destinations who had expertise in subjects we were curious to learn more about, or how to connect with other travelers who had made journeys similar to ours and had related interests. All of this would provide us a chance to expand our explorations and make us more motivated to want to revisit again and again the special places that originally intrigued us so that we could dig deeper into our topics of interest.

Thus, returning home from trips would not have to represent an end for us as much as it could be an opportunity for new beginnings. Our trips change us and help us to see the world in different ways, and travel providers could work with us to be a springboard in this growth process. In this way, the relationship forged between our travel providers and us would not have to come to an end when our trips were officially over, but could continue to evolve and deepen over time (Noy 2004) as we sought out new knowledge and experiences.

The Enduring Moment

In all of the preceding examples, we have seen how travel experiences can add a kind of richness and freshness to our lives that is not often found through other pursuits. This is the magic that travel at its best offers us. Travel experiences, especially when we continue to build on them when we return from our journeys, tend to be quite enduring and this gives us a double bonus. This is so because the pleasure gained from having rich experiences has the capacity to not just stay fresh in our minds but actually to increase over time and get deeper (Trope and Liberman 2003). As an example of this on a personal note, I can well remember my parents telling me tales about the country of Panama when I was a child. Both of my parents had served in Panama in the Second World War and met and married there. They both retained an ongoing interest in all things related to Panama for the rest of their lives and continued to learn about the country long after their direct association with it had ended. This interest was passed on to me as well. It seemed that with each re-telling of their time together there and their re-showing of their souvenirs from this period of their life, their adventures grew more wonderful and glorious and intriguing to me. It got to the point that when my father would say, "Well, when your mother and I were in Panama," I knew that a magical story and wonderful reminisces were to follow.

So it was not just the experience of being in Panama that left a deep impression on my father. Rather, it was also the joy he received from continuing to acquire knowledge about this part of the world when he returned home and his ability to relive his experiences there that added to his sense of well-being and satisfaction (Carter and Gilovich 2010). This is travel's lasting gift.

Questions for Discussion

Please reflect on the following questions to think more about how post-trip learning can enhance the joy that travel can provide. As you do this, draw on your own personal experience as a traveler and/or on any experiences you have had in the travel industry.

1. Did you ever find some new area of interest during a trip that you decided to pursue and further explore after you returned home? If yes, what were some of these new areas, and how did you continue to explore them? What was the impact of doing this?

2. What sort of follow-up information would you like to receive from travel providers about sites or places that you visited on your trips to help you in your continued exploration process? Have you ever received this sort of information? If yes, what was its impact?

3. What does the notion of travel being a portal to a new way of seeing life and living mean to you? Do you have any personal experience with this? Explain.

4. Finally, can you think of any travel memories you have had that left particularly enduring impressions in your mind? If yes, please describe these experiences. What made them so special to you?

Notes

_____

_____

_____

_____

_____

_____

Case Study 3:
Post-Trip Well-Being

You have read how a variety of techniques can be used to enhance post-trip memories and reflections. Now you will have a chance to apply some of the ideas presented in Part III of the book to a hypothetical case study. Doing this will allow you to more actively work with the concepts you have learned about and to integrate them more effectively to solve real-life type travel dilemmas. As before, there are no right or wrong answers, so do not be held back by searching for the so-called right solution. Just draw on your own experiences and use the frameworks that were provided to you to try to critically analyze the case. This case is called *Your Ski Vacation*.

Your Ski Vacation

For this exercise, imagine that you are in the middle of a one-week trip to a ski lodge in Austria. Although you had never skied before, the lodge where you are staying offered a beginner's course in skiing, which you are taking along with five other guests at the lodge. This course is turning out to be enormous fun for you, although you are not really learning to ski very well. The lodge has a pub restaurant on the premises, and every night they have what they call *Singing Evenings* where all of the guests gather by the fire and are led in song by the owner of the hotel who is an accomplished folk singer. You have attended all of these sing-alongs and are having a great time, in general, on this trip. The food has been fantastic and the conversation with other guests has been lively. Because of all of this, you want to be able to particularly savor and relish the memories of your special vacation when you return home.

Using the information presented in the preceding chapters in Part III on enhancing post-trip reflections and your own experience as a traveler or travel professional, brainstorm about *all* the things that you could do to refresh your later memories of this wonderful trip. What specific strategies would you employ to facilitate this? What types of things could you do or what could you collect or gather to preserve the freshness of your experiences? How could the lodge managers and other people in the travel industry whom you met on your trip help you in this task? Please discuss and be as specific as you can in your responses. Again there are no correct or incorrect answers.

Notes

_____

_____

_____

_____

_____

_____

The End

To travel is to live.

—Hans Christian Andersen

We will end as we began with our elusive desire for the *perfect* trip. Although the specific mode and style of our travel may change in the future, our wanderlust to explore our world will probably never end. And we know that travel, when it is done well, has the power to positively change our lives.

But is the search for the so-called perfect trip the right way to ponder the notion of what traveling well means? Good trips do not always result from traveling big or going first class or picking the most beautiful room accommodations. It is, as we have seen, more about what we *do* on our trips and how we deal with things, rather than in what surroundings we happen to find ourselves that contribute most to our sense of contentment. It is our readiness to attend to our environment and our openness to the experiences that we encounter that add to travel joy and satisfaction. All of these mindsets and attitudes can be facilitated by the travel providers with whom we work.

To consider this, we might think about successful trips we have had in our own lives. What elements did they contain? Were these trips ones in which we felt both energized and re-invigorated by our environment because we had worked with someone to plan a trip that was well paced and was neither too ambitious nor too under scheduled for us? Were they trips in which we were provided with activities that truly engaged and interested us, but also with opportunities to be able to be completely restored when we felt the need for rest? On these trips, did we feel in sync with our circumstances because our trips matched our styles and personalities and made us sense that we were in just the right sort of situation for us?

The above questions move us to frameworks for evaluating travel that concern process more than product, and that stress the nature of our interactions more than the physical attributes of our surroundings. It is, as we have talked about so much in this book, the small moments of pleasure and our receptiveness to our surroundings that in the end are most important to our trip success or failure.

To think about this from a slightly different angle, imagine a baby in a crib whose relatives brought over a new fancy mobile to place over the crib. The mobile played music as the shapes that were attached to it dangled and sparkled. In some cases, the baby might smile when she saw the mobile and wave her arms in delight. In other situations, if she was sleepy or hungry or fussy, she might ignore the mobile or even find it irritating, or she might have initially liked it but grew bored with it as it endlessly twirled hour after hour above her head. And, finally, in some scenarios, the baby may have hated the mobile from the start simply because she likes fuzzy things better than things that sparkle. So if we looked back and asked if this was a perfect mobile, we might be hard pressed to know how to answer. But we can say with certainty that it was right for some babies in some circumstances at some moments. And, clearly, the more the relatives knew the particular quirks and preferences of this baby and the more they were attuned to her psychological dispositions and current circumstances, the more successful it probably would have been as a toy.

Our situation when we travel is in many ways analogous to the situation of the small baby with the toy mobile. We, similar to the baby, have to learn to see and appreciate and savor what wonders are offered to us in our world, but, just like the baby's relatives, those who serve us have to be sensitive to our needs, preferences, current dispositions, and our tendency to sometimes get bored with our circumstances.

Creating successful travel encounters, thus, offers both challenges and opportunities for travelers and for those who work in the travel industry. It is, as we have seen, the unscripted moments, the small gestures, and the unexpected acts of thoughtfulness that tend to remain with us. It is that sense of *just rightness* that wakes us up and revitalizes us. When this *just rightness* is achieved, travel becomes an experience to be truly relished. It becomes, that is, the perfect trip that we all had in mind when we started out!

References

Adams, R.L. 2016. "Top Travel Websites for Planning Your Next Adventure." *Forbes,* March 29, 2016.

Adler, H., and S. Gordon. 2013. "An Analysis of the Changing Roles of Hotel Concierges." *Journal of Tourism and Hospitality Management* 1, no. 2, pp. 53–66.

Allen. Summer. 2018. "The Science of Awe." A White Paper Prepared for the John Templeton Foundation by the Greater Good Science Center at U.C. Berkeley.

Amabile, T., and S. Kramer. 2011. "Four Reasons to Keep a Work Diary." http://hbr.org/2011/04/four-reasons-to-keep-a-work-diary

Andersen, V., R. Prentice, and K. Watanabe. 2000. "Journeys for Experiences: Japanese Independent Travellers in Scotland." *Journal of Travel and Tourism Marketing* 9, pp. 129–151.

Ariely, D., E. Kamenica, and D. Prelac. 2008. "Man's Search for Meaning: The Case of Lagos." *Journal of Economic Behavior and Organization* 67, nos. 2–4, pp. 671–677.

Bare. S.K., and D. Bare. 2017. *Before You Go Abroad Handbook: Over 127 Secret Tips and Tools for International Travel, Book 1.* Scotts Valley, CA: Create Space Independent Publishing.

Barth, F.D. 2018. "Keeping a Journal Can Be Good for Your Emotional Health." http://psychologytoday.com/us/blog/the.couch/201805/keeping-journal-can-be-good-your-emotional-health

Baskerville, K., K. Johnson, E. Monk-Turner, Q. Slone, H. Standley, S. Stansbury, M. Williams, and Y. Young. 2000. "Reactions to Random Acts of Kindness." *The Social Science Journal* 37, no. 2, pp. 293–398.

Bickenbach, J. 2017. "WHO's Definition of Health: Philosophical Analysis." In *Handbook of the Philosophy of Medicine,* eds. T. Schramme and S. Edwards, 961–974. New York, NY: Springer.

Boothby, E., M.S. Clark, and J. Bargh. 2014. "Shared Experiences are Amplified." *Psychological Science* 25, no. 12, pp. 2209–2216.

Bowen, D., and J. Clarke. 2009. *Contemporary Tourist Behavior: Yourself and Others as Tourists.* Wallingford, ENG: CABI Publications.

Bryant, F., and J. Veroff. 2007. *Savoring: A New Model of Positive Experience.* Mahwah, NJ: Lawrence Erlbaum Associates, Inc.

Bryant, F.B., E. Chadwick, and K. Kluwe. 2011. "Understanding the Processes that Regulate Positive Emotional Experience: Unsolved Problems and Future Directions for Theory and Research on Savoring." *International Journal of Wellbeing* 1, no. 1, 107–126.

Burt, J.J. 1994. "Identity Primes Produce Facilitation in a Colour Naming Task." *Quarterly Journal of Experimental Psychology* 47A, pp. 957–1000.

Cacioppo, J.T., and R.E. Petty. 1982. "The Need for Cognition." *Journal of Personality and Social Psychology* 42, no. 1, pp. 116–131.

Cantril, H., and G.W. Allport. 1933. "Recent Applications of the Study of Values." *Journal of Abnormal and Social Psychology* 28, no. 3, pp. 259–273.

Caprariello, P.A., and H.T. Reis. 2013. "To Do, To Have or To Share? Valuing Experiences Over Material Possessions Depends on the Involvement of Others." *Journal of Personality and Social Psychology* 104, no. 2, pp. 199–215.

Carpenter, S. 2001. "A New Reason for Keeping a Diary." *American Psychological Society Monitor* 32, no. 8, p. 68.

Carter, T.J., and T. Gilovich. 2010. "The Relative Relativity of Experiential and Material Purchases." *Journal of Personality and Social Psychology* 98, no. 1, pp. 146–159.

Carter, T.J., and T. Gilovich. 2012. "I Am What I Do Not What I Have: The Differential Centrality of Experimental and Material Purchases to the Self." *Journal of Personality and Social Psychology* 102, no. 6, pp. 1304–1317.

Cary, S.H. 2004. "The Tourist Moment." *Annals of Tourism Research* 31, no. 1, pp. 61–77.

Cassidy, S. 2004. "Learning Styles: An Overview of Theories and Models and Measures." *Educational Psychology* 24, no. 4, pp. 419–444.

Cheek, N., and B. Schwartz. 2016. "On the Meaning and Measurement of Maximization." *Judgment and Decision Making* 11, no. 2, pp. 126–146.

Chen, Y., B. Mak, and B. McKercher. 2011. "What Drives People to Travel: Integrating the Tourist Motivation Paradigms." *Journal of China Tourism Research* 7, no. 2, pp. 120–136.

Chiasson, G. 2010. "Digital Photo Frames Enhance Hotel Guest Experience." http://dailydooh.com/archives/23833

Coleman, J. 1988. "Social Capital in the Creation of Human Capital." *American Journal of Sociology* 94, pp. 95–120.

Collins. R.L. 1996. "For Better or Worse: The Impact of Upward Social Comparisons on Self-Evaluations." *Psychological Bulletin* 119, no. 1, pp. 51–69.

Costa, P.T., and R.R. McCrae. 1988. "From Catalog to Classification: Murray's Needs and the Five-Factor Model of Personality." *Journal of Personality and Social Psychology* 35, no. 2, pp. 258–265.

Crompton, J. 1979. "Motivations for Pleasure Travel." *Annals of Tourism Research* 6, no. 4, pp. 408–424.

Cruz-Milan. O. 2018. "Plog's Model of Personality-Based Psychographic Traits in Tourism: A Review of Empirical Research." In *Tourist Planning and Destination Marketing*, ed. M.A. Camilleri, 49–74. Somerville, MA: Emerald Publication.

Csikszentmihaly, M., and J. Coffey. 2016. "Why Do We Travel: A Positive Psychological Model for Travel Motivation." In *Positive Tourism (Routledge Advances in Tourism)*, eds. S. Filep, J. Laing, and M. Csikszentmihaly, 2994–3004. London, UK: Routledge.

Csikszentmihalyi, M. 1990. *Flow: The Psychology of Optimal Experience.* New York, NY: Harper & Row.

CSPonline. 2016. "Communication Strategies for Great Leadership." http://online. csp.edu/blog/business/communication-strategies-for-great-leadership/

Dann, G.M. 1981. "Tourist Motivation: An Appraisal." *Annals of Tourism Research* 8, no. 2, pp. 187–219.

Davidson-Hunt, I., and F. Berkes. 2003. "Learning as You Journey: Anishinaabe Perception of Social-Ecological Environments and Adaptive Learning." *Conservation Ecology* 8, no. 1, p. 5.

Delle Fave, A., I. Brdar, T. Freire, D. Vella-Brodrick, and M. Wissing. 2011. "The Eudamonic and Hedonic Components of Happiness: Qualitative and Quantitative Findings." *Social Indicators Research* 100, no. 2, pp. 185–207.

Desforges, L. 2000. "Traveling the World: Identity and Travel Biography." *Annals of Tourism Research* 27, no. 4, pp. 926–945.

Diener, E., and M. Seligman. 2002. "Very Happy People." *Psychological Science* 13, no. 1, pp. 81–84.

Diener, E., R.L. Larsen, and R.A. Emmons. 1984. "Person-Situation Interaction: Choices of Situation and Congruence Response Models." *Journal of Personality and Social Psychology* 47, no. 3, pp. 580–592.

DiPirro, D. 2013. "Anticipation: How to Make the Most of Expectation." http://positivelypresent.com/2013/05/anticipation.html

"Digital Memories: Travel Trends in the Age of Social Media." 2018. http://storyful.com/wp-content/uploads/2019/12/Storyful-White-Paper-Travel-September-2018.pdf

Do, A.M., A.V. Rupert, and G. Wolford. 2008. "Evaluation of Pleasurable Experiences: The Peak-End Rule." *Psychonomic Bulletin and Review* 15. no. 1, pp. 96–98.

Doherty, D. 2018. "The Guide to Becoming a Vlogger in 2020." https://engagelive.co/guide-becoming-vlogger-2018/

Dube, L., and J.L. Le Bel. 2001. "A Differential View of Pleasure: Review of the Literature and Research Propositions." In *European Advances in Consumer Research Volume 5*, eds. A. Groeppel-Klein and F.R. Esch, 222–226. Provo, UT: Association for Consumer Research.

Dunn, E., and M. Norton. 2014. *Happy Money: The Science of Smarter Spending.* New York, NY. Simon Schuster.

Elkins, D.N. 2001. "Reflections on Mystery and Awe." *The Psychotherapy Patient* 11, no. 3–4, pp. 163–168.

Festinger, L. 1954. "A Theory of Social Comparison Processes." *Human Relations* 7, no. 2, pp. 117–140.

Filep, S., J. Laing, and M. Csikszentmihalyi, eds. 2016. *Positive Tourism (Routledge. Advances in Tourism Book 38)*. Abingdon, UK: Routledge.

Filep, S., J. Macnaughton, and T. Glover. 2017. "Tourism and Gratitude: Valuing Acts of Kindness." *Annals of Tourism Research* 66, pp. 26–36.

Filep. S., and P. Pearce, eds. 2014. *Tourist Experiences and Fulfillment: Insights from Positive Psychology*. Abingdon, UK: Routledge.

Fletcher, J. 2020. "10 Tips for Getting Over Jet Lag." http://medicalnewstoday.com/articles/how-to-get-over-jet-lag

Fox, A. 2019. "Travelers Will Spend 60% More Money This Year on Holidays Than Last Year According to Trivago." http://fox10tv.com/video_magazines/travel_and_leisure/traveler-will-spend-more-this-year-on-holiday.

Frederick, S., and G. Loewenstein. 1999. "Hedonic Adaptation." In *Well-being: The Foundation of Hedonic Psychology*, eds. D. Kahneman, E. Diener and N. Schwartz, 302–329. New York, NY: Russell Sage.

Fridgen, J.D. 1984. "Environmental Psychology and Tourism." *Annals of Tourism Research* 11, no. 1, pp. 19–39.

Gable, S., and J. Haidt. 2005. "What (and Why) Is Positive Psychology?" *Review of General Psychology* 9, no. 2, pp. 103–110.

Galante, J., I. Galante, M.J. Bekkers, and J. Gallacher. 2014. "Effects of Kindness-Based Meditation on Health and Well-being: A Systematic Review and Meta-analysis." *Journal of Consulting and Clinical Psychology* 82, no. 6, pp. 1101–1114.

Gilbert, D. 2007. *Stumbling on Happiness*. New York, NY: Vintage Books.

Glenville-Cleave, B. 2013. "Five Reasons to Focus on Flow." https://positivepsychologynews.com/news/bridget-grenville-cleave/2013022625517

Govindji, R., and, P.A. Linley. 2007. "Strengths Use, Self-Concordance and Well-being: Implications for Strengths Coaching and Coaching Psychologists." *International Coaching Psychology Review* 2, no. 2, pp. 143–153.

Griffith, D.A., and P.J. Albanese, 1996. "An Examination of Plog's Psychographic Travel Model with a Student Population." *Journal of Travel Research* 34, no. 4, pp. 47–51.

Hague, A. 2016. "What Does a Travel Planner Do?" https://travel4allseasonsmagazine.com/2016/06/16/what-does-a-travel-planner-do

Hammitt, W.E. 1980. "Outdoor Recreation: Is It a Multiphase Experience?" *Journal of Leisure Research* 12, no. 2, pp. 107–115.

Henik, A., F.J. Friedrich, and W.A. Kellog. 1983. "The Dependence of Semantic Relatedness Effects Upon Prime Processing." *Memory and Cognition* 11, no. 4, pp. 366–373.

"Hotels Finding Ways to Influence and Share Guests' Photos." 2018. http://hotelnewsnow.com/Articles/286451/hotels-finding-ways-to-influence-share-guests-photos

Howell, R.T., and G. Hill. 2009. "The Mediators of Experiential Purchases: Determining the Impact of Psychological Needs Satisfaction and Social Comparison." *Journal of Positive Psychology* 4, no. 6, pp. 511–522.

Hughes, J., and A.A. Scholer. 2017. "When Wanting the Best Goes Right or Wrong: Distinguishing Between Adaptive and Maladaptive Maximization." *Personality and Social Psychology Bulletin* 43, no. 4, pp. 570–583.

"Instagram Best Practices - 8 Content Tricks Used by Top Brands." 2020. http://hi.photoslurp.com/blog/instagram-best-practices-content/

Iyengar, S.S. 2011. *The Art of Choosing.* New York, NY: Twelve Publishers (Reprint Edition).

Iyengar, S.S., and M.P. Lepper. 1999. "Rethinking the Value of Choice: A Cultural Perspective on Intrinsic Motivation." *Journal of Personality and Social Psychology* 76, pp. 349–366.

Iyengar, S.S., R.E. Wells, and B. Schwartz. 2006. "Doing Better but Feeling Worse: Looking for the Best Job Undermines Satisfaction." *Psychological Science* 17, no. 2, pp. 143–150.

Iyengar, S.S., and M.R. Lepper. 2000. "When Choice is Demotivating: Can One Desire Too Much of a Good Thing?" *Journal of Personality and Social Psychology* 79, no. 6, pp. 349–366.

Jackson, S.A. 1992. "Athletes in Flow: A Qualitative Investigation of Flow State in Elite Figure Skaters." *Journal of Applied Sport Psychology* 4, no. 2, pp. 161–180.

Jani, D. 2014. "Relating Travel Personality to the Big Five Factors of Personality." *Tourism: An International Interdisciplinary Journal* 62, no. 4, pp. 347–359.

John, O.P., L.P. Naumann, and C.J. Soto. 2008. "Paradigm Shift in the Integrative Big Five Trait Taxonomy: History, Measurement and Conceptual Issues." In *Handbook of Personality: Theory and Research,* 3rd ed., eds. O.P. John, R.W. Robins and L.A. Pervin, 114–158. New York, NY: Guilford Press.

Kahle, L. 1983. "Dialectical Tensions in the Theory of Social Values." In *Social Values and Social Change: Adaptation to Life in America,* ed. L. Kahle, 275–284. New York, NY: Prager.

Kasser, T., and R. Ryan. 1996. "Further Examining the American Dream: Differential Correlates of Intrinsic and Extrinsic Goals." *Personality and Social Psychology Bulletin* 22, no. 3, pp. 280–287.

Keltner, D., and J. Haidt. 2003. "Approaching Awe: A Moral, Spiritual and Aesthetic Emotion." *Cognition and Emotions* 17, no. 2, pp. 297–314.

Koncul, N. 2012. "Wellness: A New Mode of Tourism." *Economic Research* 25, no. 2, pp. 525–534.

Kosinski, M., D. Stillwell, and T. Graepel. 2013. "Private Traits and Attributes are Predictable from Digital Recordings of Human Behavior." *Proceedings of the National Academy of Science* 110, no. 15, pp. 5802–5805.

Krause, N., and R.D. Hayward. 2014. "Assessing Whether Practical Wisdom and Awe of God are Associated with Life Satisfaction." *Psychology of Religion and Spirituality* 7, no. 1, pp. 51–59.

Kringelbach, M.L., and K.C. Berridge. 2010. "The Neuroscience of Happiness and Pleasure." *Social Research* 77, no. 2, pp. 659–678.

Kumar, A., and T. Gilovich. 2015. "Some 'Thing' to Talk About? Differential Story Utility from Experiential and Material Purchases." *Personality and Social Psychology Bulletin* 41, no. 10, pp. 1320–1331.

Kumar, A., M.A. Killingsworth, and T. Gilovich. 2014. "Waiting for Merlot: Anticipating Consumption of Experiential and Material Purchases." *Psychological Science* 25, no. 10, pp. 1924–1931.

Kurtz, J. 2017. *The Happy Traveler: Unpacking the Secrets of Better Vacations.* New York, NY: Oxford University Press.

Lakein. A. 1974. *How to Get Control of your Time and Your Life.* New York, NY: The New American Library (NAL).

Larsen, J., P. McGraw, and J.T. Cacioppo. 2001. "Can People Feel Happy and Sadat the Same Time?" *Journal of Personality and Social Psychology* 81, no. 4, pp. 684–696.

Larsen, J.T., and A.R. McKibban. 2008. "Is Happiness Having What You Want, Wanting What You Have, or Both? *Psychological Science* 19, no. 4, pp. 371–377.

Le Bel, J.L., and L. Dube. 2001. "The Impact of Sensory Knowledge and Attentional Focus on Pleasure and Behavioral Responses to Hedonic Stimuli." Paper presented at the 13th American Psychological Association Convention. Toronto, Canada.

Levine, D. 2018. "Can You Boost Your Mental Health by Keeping a Journal?" http://health.usnews.com/health-care/patient-advice/articles/2018-09-24/can-you-boost-your-mental-health-by-keeping-a-journal

Litvin, S. 2006. "Revisiting Plog's Model of Allocentricity and Psychocentricity... One More Time." *Cornell Hospitality Quarterly* 47, no. 3, pp. 245–253.

Luna, T. 2015. "Surprise! Why the Unexpected Feels Good, and Why It's Good for Us." http://wnycstudios.org/podcasts/takeaway/segments/surprise-unexpected-why-it-feels-good-and-why-its-good-us

Mackenzie, S.H., and J.H. Kerr. 2013. "Stress and Emotions at Work: An Adventure Tourism Guide to Experiences." *Tourism Management* 36, pp. 3–14.

Maslow, A. 1943. "A Theory of Human Motivation." *Psychological Review* 50, no. 4, pp. 370–396.

Maslow, A. 1968. *Toward a Psychology of Being,* 2nd ed. New York, NY: Van Nostrand Reinhold Company Inc.

Massimini, F., and M. Carli. 1988. "The Systematic Assessment of Flow in Daily Experience." In *Optimal Experience,* eds. M. Csikszentmihalyi and I. Csikszentmihalyi, 266–287. New York, NY: Cambridge University Press.

Matz, S., and O. Netzer. 2017. "Using Big Data as a Window into Consumers' Psychology." *Current Opinion in Behavioral Sciences* 18, pp. 7–12.

McCrae, R.R. 2004. "Conscientiousness." In *Encyclopedia of Applied Psychology*, ed. C. Spielberger, 469–472. Boston, MA: Elsevier Academic Press.

McGrath, R.E., and N. Wallace. 2021. "Cross-validation of the VIA Inventory of Strengths and Its Short Forms." *Journal of Personality Assessment* 103, no. 1, pp. 120–131.

Mikula, G., B. Petri, and N. Tanzer. 1990. "What People Regard as Unjust: Types and Structures of Everyday Experiences of Injustice." *European Journal of Social Psychology* 20, no. 2, pp. 133–149.

Moneta, G., and M. Csikszentmihalyi. 1996. "The Effect of Perceived Challenges and Skills on the Quality of Subjective Experience." *Journal of Personality* 64, no. 2, pp. 275–310.

Morris, J. 2019. "User-Generated Content & the Hospitality Industry: An Incredible Marketing Strategy." https://taggbox.com/ blog/ugc-for-hospitality-industry/

Moscardo, G. 2011. "Searching for Well-being: Exploring Change in Tourist Motivation." *Tourism Recreation Research* 36, no. 1, pp. 15–26.

Mossberg, L. 2007. "A Marketing Approach to the Tourist Experience." *Scandinavian Journal of Hospitality and Tourism* 7, no.1, pp. 59–74.

Mueller, H., and E. Kaufmann. 2001. "Wellness Tourism: Market Analysis of a Special Health Tourism Segment and Implications for the Hotel Industry." *Journal of Vacation Marketing* 7, no. 1, pp. 5–17.

Nawijn, J., M.A. Marchand, R. Veenhoven, and A.J. Vingerhoets. 2010. "Vacationers Happier, but Most Not Happier After a Holiday." *Applied Research in Quality of Life* 5, no. 1, pp. 35–47.

Noone, B.M., S.E. Kimes, A.S. Mattila, and J. Wirtz. 2007. "The Effects of Meal Pace on Customer Satisfaction." *The Cornell Hotel and Restaurant Association Quarterly* 48, no. 3, pp. 231–244.

Noy, C. 2004. "This Trip Really Changed Me: Backpackers' Narratives of Self-Change." *Annals of Tourism Research* 31, no. 1, pp. 78–102.

O'Donnell, J. 2015. "17 Facts about New Mexico You Never Would have Guessed." https://matadornetwork.com/notebook/17-facts-new-mexico-never-guessed/

Opperman, M. 1995. "Destination Threshold Potential and the Law of Repeat Visitations." *Annals of Tourism Research* 22, pp. 535–552.

Otake, K., S. Shimai, J. Tanaka-Matsumi, K. Otsui, and B.L. Fredrickson. 2006. "Happy People Become Happier Through Kindness: A Counting Kindness Intervention." *Journal of Happiness Studies* 7, no. 3, pp. 361–375.

Patel, N. 2015. "The Psychology of Excitement: How to Better Engage Your Audience." http://blog.hubspot.com/marketing/psychology-of-excitetment

Pearce, P.L., S. Filep, and G. Ross. 2011. *Tourists, Tourism and the Good Life*. New York, NY: Routledge.

Pearce, P.L. 2005. *Tourist Behavior: Themes and Conceptual Schemes*. Bristol, EN: Channel View Publications.

Pearce, P.L., and F. Foster. 2007. "A University of Travel: Backpacker Learning." *Tourism Management* 28, pp. 1285–1298.

Pervin, L.A. 1989. *Personality Theory and Research,* 5th ed. New York, NY: John Wiley.

Peterson, C., and M. Seligman. 2004. *Character Strengths and Virtues: A Handbook of Classification*. New York, NY: Oxford University Press.

Pine, B.J., and J.H. Gilmore. 1998. "Welcome to the Experience Economy." *Harvard Business Review* 76, no. 4, pp. 97–105.

Pine, B.J., and J.H. Gilmore. 2019. *The Experience Economy, with a New Preface by the Author: Competing for Customer Time, Attention and Money.* Cambridge, MA: Harvard Business Review Press.

Plog, S.C. 1974. "Why Destination Areas Rise and Fall in Popularity." *The Cornell Hospitality Quarterly* 14, no. 4, pp. 55–58.

Plog, S.C. 1991. *Leisure Travel : Making It a Growth Market...Again!*. New York, NY: John Wiley.

Plog, S.C. 2001. "Why Destination Areas Rise and Fall in Popularity: An Update of a Cornell Quarterly Classic." *The Cornell Hotel and Restaurant Quarterly* 42, no. 3, pp. 13–24.

Plog, S.C. 2002. "The Power of Psychographics and the Concept of Venturesomeness." *Journal of Travel Research* 40, no. 3, pp. 244–251.

Pressman, S.D., K.A. Matthews, S. Cohen, L. M. Martire, M. Scheier, and A. Baum. 2009. "Association of Enjoyable Leisure Activities with Psychological and Physical Well-being." *Psychosomatic Medicine* 71, no. 7, pp. 725–732.

Quoidbach, J., M. Mikolajczak, and J.J. Gross. 2015. "Positive Interventions: An Emotional Regulation Perspective." *Psychological Bulletin,* 141, no. 3, pp. 655–693.

Rammstedt, B., and O.P. John. 2007. "Measuring Personality in One Minute or Less: A 10 Item Short Version of the Big Five Inventory in English and German." *Journal of Research in Personality* 41, p. 210.

Rashid, T. 2015. "Positive Psychotherapy: A Strength-based Approach." *The Journal of Positive Psychology* 10, no. 1, pp. 25–40.

Rettner, R. 2010. "Brain's Links Between Sounds, Smells and Memory Revealed." http://livescience.com/8426-brain-link-sounds-smells-memory-revealed

ReviewPro. 2019. "The Pros and Cons of Hotel Loyalty Programs." http://reviewpro.com/blog/pros-cons-loyalty-programs/

Rigoglioso, M. 2008. "Research Confirms: It's the Thought That Counts." https://gsb.stanford.edu/insights/research-confirms-its-thought-counts

Roberts, W. 2014. "The Joy of Anticipation." http://psychologies.co.uk/self/life-lab-experiment-mind-2html

Rokeach, M. 1979. "From Individual to Institutional Values with Special Reference to the Values of Science." In *Understanding Human Values: Individual and Societal*, ed. M. Rokeach, 47–70. New York, NY: The Free Press.

Roser, M. 2020. "Tourism." http://ourworldindata.org/tourism

Schmitt, B.H. 2003. *Customer Experience Management: A Revolutionary Approach to Connecting with Your Customer*. New York, NY: John Wiley & Sons.

Schueller, S.M. 2014. "Person-Activity Fit in Positive Psychological Interventions." In *The Wiley Blackwell Handbook of Positive Psychological Interventions*, eds. A Parks and S.M. Schueller, 385–403, West Sussex, UK: John Wiley and Sons.

Seligman, M.E. 2002. *Authentic Happiness*. New York, NY: Simon Schuster.

Seligman, M.E. 2011. *Flourish: A Visionary New Understanding of Happiness*. New York, NY: Free Press.

Seligman, M.E. 2012. *Flourish: A Visionary New Understanding of Happiness and Well-being*. New York, NY: The Free Press.

Selstad, L. 2007. "The Social Anthropology of the Tourist Experience: Exploring the 'Middle Role'." *Scandinavian Journal of Hospitality and Management* 7, no. 1, pp. 19–33.

Seltzer. L.F. 2017. "Feeling Understood Even More Important Than Feeling Loved." http://psychologytoday.com/us/blog/evolution-the-self/201706/feeling-understood-even-more-important-feeling-loved

Shashou, A. April 17, 2017. "4 Ways Concierges Can Use Technology to Craft the Guest Experience." https://hotel-online.com/pressrelease/4-ways-concierges-can-use-technology-to-craft-the-guest-experience

Sheldon, K.M., and A.J. Elliot. 1999. "Goal Striving, Need Satisfaction and Longitudinal Well-Being: The Self-Concordance Model." *Journal of Personality and Social Psychology* 76, no. 3, pp. 482–497.

Shiota, M.N., D.J. Keltner, and A. Steiner. 2007. "The Nature of Awe: Elicitors, Appraisals, and Effects on Self-Concept." *Cognition and Emotion* 21, no. 5, pp. 944–963.

Shulman, N. 1992. *Zen and the Art of Climbing Mountains*. Boston, MA: Charles E. Tuttle Press.

Skinner, J., and D. Theodossopoulos. 2011. *Great Expectation : Imagination and Anticipation in Tourism*. New York, NY: Berghahn Books.

Smith, M., and L. Puczko. 2009. *Health and Wellness Tourism*. London: Butterworth-Heinemann.

Smith, S.L.J. 1990. "A Test of Plog's Model: Evidence from Seven Nations." *Journal of Travel Research* 28, pp. 40–43.

Soni, D. 2019. *An Introduction to the Big Five Theories of Personality, Kindle Edition*, Amazon.com Services, LLC.

Srivastava, S. 2021. "Measuring the Big Five Personality Domains." http://pages
.uoregon.edu/sanjay/bigfive.html

Stephens, R. September, 2020. "Dive Into Your Own Private Pool in these Luxe
Hotel Rooms." http://lonelyplanet.com/articles/hotels-with-private-plunge-
pools

Strati, A., D.J. Shernoff, and H.Z. Kackar. 2012. "Flow." In *Encyclopedia of
Adolescence*, ed. R. Levesque, 1050–1059. New York, NY: Springer.

Stylianou-Lambert, T. 2012. "Tourists with Cameras: Reproducing or Producing."
Annals of Tourism Research 39, no. 4, pp. 1817–1838.

Sutton, R. 1992. "Feelings About a Disneyland Visit: Photographs and
Reconstruction of Bygone Emotions." *Journal of Management Inquiry* 1,
no. 4, pp. 278–287.

Terra, J. 2020. "GDPR and What It Means for Big Data." http://simplilearn.com/
search?tag=GDPR+and+what+it+means+for+big+data#/item_type=course,
bundle

Trope, Y., and N. Liberman. 2003. "Temporal Construal." *Psychological Review*
110, no. 3, pp. 403–421.

UNWTO. 2019. "Exports from International Travel Hit USD 1.7 Trillion."
http://unwto.org/global/press-release/2019-06-06/exports-international-
tourism-hit-usd-1.7-trillion

UNWTO. 2020. "World Tourism Barometer No. 18 January 2020." http://
unwto.org/world-tourism-barometer-n18-january-2020

Van Boven, L., and T. Gilovich. 2003. "To Do or To Have? That is the Question."
Journal of Personality and Social Psychology 85, no. 6, pp. 1193–1202.

Walker, W.R., J.J. Skowronski, and C.P. Thompson. 2003. "Life is Pleasant - and
Memory Helps Keep It That Way." *Review of General Psychology* 7, no. 2,
pp. 203–210.

Walster, E., G.W. Walster, and E.S. Berscheid. 1978. *Equity Theory and Research*,
MA: Boston, MA: Allen and Bacon.

Wang, N. 1999. "Rethinking Authenticity in Tourism Experiences." *Annals of
Tourism Research* 26, no. 2, pp. 349–370.

Waterman. A. 2008. "Reconsidering Happiness: A Eudaimonist's Perspective."
Journal of Positive Psychology 3, no. 4, pp. 234–252.

Wedel, M., and P.K. Kannan. 2016. "Marketing Analytics for Data-Rich
Environments." *Journal of Marketing* 80, no. 6, pp. 97–121.

Weiss, L. 2016. "5 Ways to Maintain Your Vacation Happiness." http://usnews.
com/topics/author/liz-weiss/2016

"What You Should Know About Offering Personal Concierge Services at
Your Hotel." 2019. https://reliablewater247.com/offering-hotel-personal-
concierge-services

Wheeler, L., and K. Miyake. 1992. "Social Comparisons in Everyday Life."
Journal of Personality and Social Psychology 62, no. 5, pp. 760–773.

Xie, P.F. 2016. "Optimal Arousal." In *Encyclopedia of Tourism,* eds. J. Jafari and H. Xiao,15–28. New York, NY: Springer.

Yeldell, R. 2017. "Big Data, Happy Guests: Using Analytics to Enhance the Guest Experience." http://business.comcast.com/community/browse-all/details/big-data-happy-guests-using-analytics-to-enhance-the-guest-experience

About the Author

Virginia Murphy-Berman received her PhD in clinical psychology from Northwestern University. She has been an active researcher and teacher in the field of psychology for over 40 years. For 12 years, she was a professor in the psychology department at Skidmore College in Saratoga Springs, NY, where she regularly taught courses on the psychology of well-being and cross-cultural psychology. Dr. Murphy-Berman has served as a reviewer for numerous journals in the field and is on two journal editorial boards. She has published over 50 articles, books, and book chapters in various areas of psychology, including two books recently published by Momentum Press: *Justice in Life and Society: How We Decide What is Fair (2016)* and *Finding Happiness: It All Depends on Your Focus (2018).* Being an avid world traveler, Dr. Murphy-Berman has had the opportunity to take numerous trips throughout the United States, Asia, and Europe, and she has lived abroad for extended periods of time in several different countries. She is currently retired and lives with her husband in Saratoga Springs, NY.

Index

Active involvement, 5
Actual trip, case study, 99–100
Allocentric travel style, 45
Allocentrics, 38
Anchoring issues, 72

Big Data approach, 44–45
Big Five Theory of Personality
  conscientiousnes, 37
  introversion/extroversion, 37, 38
  openness, 37
  traits, 36

Caring attitude, 78
Character virtues and strengths,
  39–40
Comfort setting options, 74
Communication patterns, 66–67
Conscientiousnes, 37
Contextual or background
  information, 25–26

Direct in-person consultations, 67
Discoverers, 24
Dreaming, 17–18

Environmental fit
  person-environment fit, 36–38
  personality and value preferences,
    43–48
Existential authenticity, 36
Experiential exercises, 27
Experiential priming, 26–27

Five-Factor Model of Personality,
  36–38
Flower arrangement, 91–92

General Data Protection Regulation
  (GDPR), 45
Grand Canyon example, 96–97

Guest loyalty programs, 75

Habituation
  act of noticing, 79–80
  acts of kindness, 78–79
  helping travelers, 73
  personalization, 74–75
  physical environment's basic
    comfort features, 74
  repeated exposure to things, 72
  surprises, 77–78
  travel options, 71–72
Health, 58
Health tourism activities, 58
Hotel amenities, 67

Introversion/extroversion, 37

Journaling
  advantages, 114
  documentary records, 113
  narratives, 115–116
  ongoing narrative reflection, 113
  reaction capture, 113–114
  reviewing, 114
  rich background information, 115
  trip impressions recording, 114,
    115

Kindness, 78–79

Maximizing tendencies, 18–19
Mementos, 103–104
Memorable experiences, 7–8
Mindfulness, 58–59

Need satisfaction, 8–9
Negative comparisons
  communication patterns, 66–67
  insidiousness, 63–65
  unfairness assessments, 65–66

Openness, 37
Optimal arousal theory, 83
Optimal functioning, 8–9

Peak and end rule, 86
Perfect trip, 123
Person-environment fit
  Big Five Theory of Personality, 36–38
  character virtues and strengths, 39–40
  existential authenticity, 36
  Plog's Model of Tourist Typology, 38–39
Personality and value preferences
  Big Data approach, 44–45
  information collection, 43–44
  travel environment, 47–48
  two travelers tale, 45–47
Physical mementos, 103
Picture post, 106
Plog's Psychographic Typology of Tourists, 38–39
Positive emotions, nature of awe, 96
Post-trip knowledge extension
  enduring moment, 119
  learning and exploring, 117–119
Post-trip well-being
  case study, 121–122
  creating scenes, 105–106
  mementos, 103–104
  recollections, 104–105
Pre-trip anticipation, 15
  case study, 50–51
  excitement
    Bayeux tapestry museum, 31–32
    Christmas memories, 30–31
    New Mexico trip planning, 30
    travel providers and enthusiasm, 32
  principles, 29
Psychocentrics, 38
Psychological dispositions, 124
Psychological flow
  conditions, 91–92
  engagement and well-being, 89–90
  flow profiles, 92–93
  flow state, 90
  helping travelers, 92–93
Psychological well-being, 8–9

Realistic trip goals, 20–21
Refresh packages, 57
Relaxation and savoring, 59
Revitalization, 58

Sanctuary environments, 58
Self-diminishing aspect of awe, 95
Self-drawings, 8
Self-expansion, 7–8
Self-transcendence, 9
Short-term restorative situations, 56–57
Social capital, 10
Self-diminishing aspect of awe, 95
Storytelling
  hotel-related travel memories, 111
  reconnection process, 110
  reconstruction process, 109–110
  reunion sessions, 111
Strength-based approach, 39–40
Successful trips, 123
Surprises, 77–78

Time pressures, 19–20
Time usage
  good pacing
    customers' desire, 85
    guided tours, 85
    power of anticipation, 85
    responsiveness, 83
    restaurant experiences, 84
  time sequencing, 86–87
Tour guide, 5
Trait theory of behavior, 36–38
Travel
  active involvement, 5
  awe nature, 95–97
  as experience, 4–5
  benefits, 7
  healing places, 4
  need satisfaction, 8–9
  purpose, 3–4
  push and pull reasons, 4
  self-expansion, 7–8
  social capital, 10
  social connections to others, 9–10
Travel fatigue
  Caribbean island trip, 56

savoring idea, 58–60
short-term, 56–57
wellness vacations, 58
Travel planners, 20–21
Trip perfection, 19
Trip planning processes
  imposed time pressures, 19–20
  maximizing tendencies, 18–19
  realistic trip goals, 20–21
  trip dreaming, 17–18
Trip readiness
  contextual or background
    information, 25–26

experiential priming, 26–27
facts and data, 23–25
practical arrangements, 23–24
preparation preference, 26

User-generated content (UGC), 106

Values, 39
Values in Action (VIA) characteristics,
  44

Wellness vacations, 58

OTHER TITLES IN THE TOURISM AND HOSPITALITY MANAGEMENT COLLECTION

Betsy Bender Stringam, New Mexico State University, Editor

- *Food and Beverage Management in the Luxury Hotel Industry* by Sylvain Boussard
- *Targeting the Mature Traveler* by Jacqueline Jeynes
- *Hospitality* by Chris Sheppardson
- *Food and Architecture* by Subhadip Majumder, and Sounak Majumder
- *A Time of Change in Hospitality Leadership* by Chris Sheppardson
- *Improving Convention Center Management Using Business Analytics and Key Performance Indicators, Volume II* by Myles T. McGrane
- *Improving Convention Center Management Using Business Analytics and Key Performance Indicators , Volume I* by Myles T. McGrane
- *A Profile of the Hospitality Industry, Second Edition* by Betsy Bender Stringam
- *Cultural and Heritage Tourism and Management* by Tammie J. Kaufman
- *Marine Tourism, Climate Change, and Resilience in the Caribbean, Volume II* by Kreg Ettenger, Samantha Hogenson, and Martha Honey
- *Marketing Essentials for Independent Lodging* by Pamela Lanier
- *Marine Tourism, Climate Change, and Resiliency in the Caribbean, Volume I* by Samantha Hogenson, and Martha Honey
- *Catering and Convention Service Survival Guide in Hotels and Casinos* by Lisa Lynn Backus, and Patti J. Shock,

Announcing the Business Expert Press Digital Library

Concise e-books business students need for classroom and research

This book can also be purchased in an e-book collection by your library as

- a one-time purchase,
- that is owned forever,
- allows for simultaneous readers,
- has no restrictions on printing, and
- can be downloaded as PDFs from within the library community.

Our digital library collections are a great solution to beat the rising cost of textbooks. E-books can be loaded into their course management systems or onto students' e-book readers.
The **Business Expert Press** digital libraries are very affordable, with no obligation to buy in future years. For more information, please visit **www.businessexpertpress.com/librarians**. To set up a trial in the United States, please email **sales@businessexpertpress.com**.

www.ingramcontent.com/pod-product-compliance
Lightning Source LLC
Chambersburg PA
CBHW061321220326
41599CB00026B/4973